Dedicated to my friend Tom
who challenged me to
write a book in a week.
And I did.

Introduction

When I was writing my first book, "365 Ways to Stop Sabotaging Your Life", I asked a couple of friends for help. Some of my friends know a lot of random facts, so I asked them to give me as many inspiring stories as possible.

One of my friends told me a story. There was a boy drowning and a farmer saved him. The drowning boy's father, Randolph, thanked the farmer by promising to pay for his son's education.

That boy was Alexander Fleming who grew up to discover penicillin.

What's more incredible is Randolph was the father of Winston Churchill.

What's even more incredible is Churchill's life was endangered years later and he was saved by penicillin.

Penicillin has saved millions of people's lives thanks to Churchill's father being at the right place at the right time.

I thought this was one of the most incredible stories I have heard in my life. It's such a brilliant example of how one act can create a cycle of positivity for decades affecting millions of lives.

I went home to research it further before I put it into my book.

But there was a problem.

It's not true.

There are so many inconsistencies in this story that it can't even be hypothetically possible. Yet people believe it because it is an uplifting story.

Also, Fleming didn't discover penicillin. Ernest Duchesne discovered it before Fleming did. He died before he could prove his discovery.

But wait a minute…he didn't discover it either! Bedouin tribesmen from North Africa have been using penicillin for millennia.

And Churchill was never saved by penicillin.

In this book, I have busted 365 myths that have been disguised as genuine information in schoolbooks, encyclopedias, and "facts" plaguing the Internet.

Hopefully, some of these will change your perception of reality for the better. Enjoy.

Content

Animals
Books
Dinosaurs
Disorders
Food and Drink
History
Human Body
Inventions
Miscellaneous
Movies
People
Places
Quotes
Religion
Science
Space
Unsolved Mysteries
Words

ANIMALS

1.   **Flamingos are pink because they eat shrimp.**
     Flamingos are pink because they eat blue-green algae (which is red, orange, and yellow.) But never pink. Or blue. Or green.
     If you think that's stupid, get used to it. You only just started this book.

2.   **The first animal to be domesticated was the dog.**
     It wasn't the dog, or the cat, or the horse, or the sheep.
     14,000 years ago, Mongolians were the first to domesticate the reindeer.

3.   **Rudolf the Red-nosed Reindeer is a boy.**
     Rudolf is female because she has antlers. Male reindeers lose their antlers in winter.

4.   **Piranhas can shred any animal to bones in less than a minute.**
     Piranhas are scared of most animals, including humans. They usually eat dead animals. Their infamous frenzies were greatly exaggerated to intrigue Western tourists.

5.   **Dogs are colorblind.**
     A dog's spectrum isn't as wide as ours but they do not see things like an old black-and-white movie. They can see blue, violet, and yellow.
     The only strong color they can't see is green but greenblind doesn't have the same ring as colorblind.

6.   **Scorpions are one of the most dangerous animals on Earth.**
     There are over a thousand types of scorpions.
     95% are harmless to humans.
     Only twenty-three people die annually from scorpion stings.

7.   **Chameleons change color to blend into their surroundings.**
     Chameleons change color to convey their mood to make them look aggressive to predators.
     The animal that blends into its surroundings the most efficiently is the octopus.

8.   Tortoises live longer than any other animal.
        Tortoises can live for over two hundred years. But nothing can compare to The Immortal Jellyfish (and its name is barely an exaggeration.) This jellyfish can revert its cells and make itself younger. There are jellyfish alive today that could potentially be ten thousand years old, if not older.

9.   The strongest animal is the ant, which can lift forty-nine times its own weight.
        The dung beetle can pull 1,141 times its own body weight. That's twenty-three times stronger than an ant.
        This would be like a human being pulling six double-decker buses full of people.

10.   All apes walk on their hands.
        Gibbons naturally walk upright like a human being.

11.   Moths are attracted to fire because they think it's the sun.
        The reason why moths act strangely near bright lights is because it makes them dizzy. They may go closer to the light out of disorientation rather than curiosity.

12.   Moths eat clothes.
        Moths never eat clothes. Their larva do. If you see a moth on an old coat and you scare it away, you may think that your coat has been saved. Unfortunately, the moth has probably laid its eggs and your coat is doomed.

13.   Turkeys can't fly.
        You would think there's no way a turkey can fly because it's too big. And that's true. But that's because turkeys are fattened up for our sake and become too fat to fly.
        Turkeys in the wild can fly at fifty-five miles per hour.

14.   When you listen to a seashell, you can hear the ocean.
        That sound is air resonating in a hollowed object. The same effect can be replicated with a cup.

15.   Sardines are a type of fish.
        Have you ever seen a sardine in the aquarium or sea or on a nature documentary? Have you ever seen a live sardine? Sardines aren't a type of fish. A tin of sardines is compromised of many types of fish and each tin can vary what types of fish it came from.

16.   Polar bears are white.
     The white color in their fur is snow. A polar bear's fur is transparent. If a polar bear was in the woods, it would look brown

17.   All polar bears are left-handed.
     This is one of those facts that you hear that sounds so random that you may think that it has to be true because no one would make up something this stupid. But they did.

18.   Polar bears are dying out because of the melting ice caps.
     As you now know, polar bears aren't white. Which means that polar bears have been spotted in areas with melted snow but people thought they were grizzly's because they were brown.

19.   Polar bears and penguins live in the same area.
     They live on opposite Poles.

20.   Most polar bears reside on the North Pole.
     Most polar bears are in Canada. There are some Canadian towns where there are as many polar bears as there are people.

21.   If a bear attacks you, play dead.
     Unless you can control your breathing perfectly while a 2,000lb pound bear is sniffing you, you are going to get ripped to shreds.
     To survive a bear attack, you need to get naked.
     Hear me out.
     Take off your shoe, place it on the ground and casually walk away. The bear will examine it for a minute. Once it looks like it's starting to get bored, take off your other shoe. Place it down, walk away for about a minute and then take off your sock and so on. Repeat this process until you are pretty naked. You should be far away, which should give you a decent head start to run.
     The only problems with this is –
     a) The bear has your scent because you gave it all of your clothes.
     b) You're naked.
     Also, you can distract a bear with toothpaste. I am not joking. They have been known to tear down cabins to devour some Colgate toothpaste. So maybe promise to give him some if he behaves.
     But the problem with that is, it'll assume you have more....and you're still naked.

22.   You can get warts from toads.
     Warts are a viral infection so a toad can't cause them.

23.   Cats should drink milk.

Cats are lactose intolerant. Milk is more damaging to a cat than seawater.

24.   If you drop a cat from a high building, it's irrelevant that it will land on its feet because it can't survive.

Cats are more likely to survive if they are thrown from the tenth story of a building than the fifth story of a building because it gives their body more time to process what's happening and adapt to it. Please don't ever test this.

25.   LOLcats are a recent fad.

If you don't know what LOLcats are…have you seen the Internet? LOLcats is an Internet meme of cats doing silly things with a funny caption. The most famous one is Grumpy Cat.

Although there has been an explosion of popularity with LOLcats in the past few years, the idea has been around since the Victorian era.

In the 1800s, Walter Potter used to dress cats up and put them in ridiculous poses and sold them as humorous postcards.

26.   Cats purr because they are happy.

Cats purr when they are ill, in pain, and even when they are dying.

Cats purr to vibrate their skeleton as a self-defense mechanism.

If you stroke a cat, it doesn't purr because it likes it; it purrs to maintain its posture. This is the reason cats rarely gets disorders like arthritis and why they are so agile and limber.

27.   Cats stroke you because they like you or they want food.

Cats don't see themselves as pets. They think that they own you. Humans feed them, stroke them, buy toys for them, and clean out their litter box. A cat strokes you to remind you that you are its property. So if a cat wants food and it starts nudging you, it's not the human version of, "Come ooonnn buddddy." It's more like, "Obey me!"

If you have a cat, have you noticed that when it comes into the house, it might suddenly act very affectionate? The cat may also do this before it ventures outside. This may be because there is an animal outside that it's scared of, so it will rub against you so you smell like the cat and the cat smells like you.

If you go outside, the predator will know that you are the cat's "protector." If the cat smells like you, the predator knows that its "protector" is near.

28.   Cats present their prey to you as a gift.
Right, at this point, you may be starting to grasp that cats don't do anything to show that they are nice. This fact will be no different.
Cats don't understand how humans have food. They can't grasp refrigerators and they have never seen you kill anything (hopefully.)
So when a cat brings you a mouse, it is not a present; it's showing you how to catch prey. Basically, it thinks you are a terrible hunter.

29.   One human year is equivalent to seven years for dogs.
It varies from dog to dog.
Even still, it's inaccurate to think that when a dog is two, it is fourteen in human terms.
Different types of dogs age differently to each other. So a small dog would be a "toddler" or "teenager" for a different length of time than a large dog.
All animals go through different stages of maturity for different lengths of time. Tortoises spend about a hundred years as a teenager (that's why they go wild and stop doing their homework.)

30.   A blue whale could swallow a car.
The blue whale's throat is only big enough to swallow a beach ball.

31.   The longest animal is the blue whale.
The longest animal is the bootlace worm. The longest one ever found was 180ft feet, nearly double the length of the blue whale.

32.   The loudest animal underwater is the blue whale.
I've decided to ruin every record the blue whale supposedly has. Groups of snapping shrimp are the loudest sound ever heard from an animal. They snap their claws in unison creating a sound that is 160 decibels. A motorcycle engine is not even half that loud. You would experience permanent ear damage if you heard this sound.

33.   Humans are the only animals that experience menopause.
Killer whales do too. Never ask how biologists found that out.

34.   Killer whales are whales.
Killer whales are dolphins…
You might think, "Impossible! Dolphins are friendly and will save humans in danger." Well…

35. Dolphins are friendly and will save humans in danger.

Dolphins are extremely intelligent like humans. And much like people, they can be nice or nasty. If you were drowning, dolphins might save you.

Or they might stab you with their snout, just for fun or to try to impress other dolphins. (Peer pressure is a big deal in the dolphin community.)

36. Dolphins drink water.

Dolphins can't drink seawater because they are mammals. Any water that goes into their mouth gets spewed out of their blowhole. A dolphin gets all of the water it needs from the fish it eats.

37. People used to use leeches for medical purposes thousands of years ago.

Leeches are still used for surgery to this day, especially for plastic surgery, osteoarthritis, severe bruising, and third-degree burns.

Not only do leeches devour an incredible amount of blood considering their small size, but their saliva has an anesthetic, so it doesn't hurt. It also has an anticoagulant so leeches can prevent blood from clotting.

There is no medical tool as convenient (and cheap) in preventing blood clotting than a leech.

38. Wolves howl at the moon.

Wolves howl to communicate with other wolves. They do this at night because they're nocturnal. They have to howl upwards because it helps project the sound. Howling up at a moon is a cool image but they won't necessarily do it in moonlight. It's not like the moon turns them violent and wild. Which reminds me...

39. The moon can turn some animals violent or wild.

There have been many stories of animals going wild after a full moon. For the longest time, nobody could figure out why.

And there is a perfect non-supernatural explanation for it.

If the moon is full, there is more light. So it's more likely that prey can see predators coming and the prey have a better chance of escaping.

Wild animals go berserk the next day because they are absolutely starving.

40.   Sharks have to keep moving or they will die.

Sharks stop moving when they sleep. The ocean current may move them but they are not making a conscious effort to move.

41.   The Great White Shark has stopped evolving.

Evolution doesn't work this way. It doesn't go, "There's nothing else to do. I'm calling it a day." All animals are constantly evolving.

42.   Sharks kill more humans than any other animal.

Sharks kill about five people a year.

Vending machines kill over twice that many. (They're notoriously sneaky.)

Humans kill 100 million sharks annually. That's three per second. If anything, sharks should be scared of us.

Hippos kill more people than any other animal, clocking up almost 3,000 kills per year (despite the fact they are vegetarian.)

Yet there is still not one single Killer Hippo Movie. Yet.

43.   Sharks can't get cancer.

The study of sharks has made huge advancements in cancer research but they are prone to cancer.

44.   Sharks are made of bone.

Sharks have no bones in their body. Their skeleton is made of cartilage.

45.   Sharks can find you from a single drop of your blood in the ocean.

This sounds like an exaggeration but it is actually an understatement.

Even if you're not bleeding, sharks can still detect where you are even if you are hundreds of meters away. Sharks are so sensitive to the ocean current that they can tell if an object (you) is interrupting its flow.

46.   The most dangerous animal in Australia is the shark.

No it isn't, and it's not a scorpion, snake, spider, or crocodile.

It's the horse. One quarter of all animal-related deaths in Australia are statistically from horses.

Surely the shark is the second most dangerous animal, right?

No. In terms of kills, that would be the cow.

Third? That's the dog.

Sharks kill slightly more people in Australia than cats.

47.   Pigs are filthy.

Pigs are one of the cleanest animals. They can't just go to sleep on the ground like most mammals. They are the only farm animal to make sleeping arrangements. They are very particular with keeping their den tidy.

So if they are not filthy, why are they always covered in mud?"

Pigs don't have sweat glands so they need to be covered in mud to keep cool or they can die from dehydration. Speaking of which...

48.   Pigs sweat.

Of all the animals on Earth, they picked the one animal that doesn't have sweat glands for the phrase "sweating like a pig."

49.   Peacocks use their tails to impress peahens.

The peacock's tail isn't used to woo females but to intimidate predators.

50.   Ostriches bury their head in the sand when threatened.

How would they breathe?

BOOKS

51.   Most fairytales like Cinderella and Snow White came from The Brothers Grimm.

The Brothers Grimm didn't make up any of the fairytales in their book. The book is simply a collection of old folk stories that originate from all over Europe (mostly Germany.) Some of the stories were written hundreds of years before The Brothers Grimm made their version.

52.   Fairytales were written for kids.

The story Rumplestilskin ends with the title character ripping his own body in half in a rage.

If you think that fairytale is bad...

53.   The Big Bad Wolf eats Red Riding Hood's grandmother.

Originally Red Riding Hood eats her own grandmother!

54.   Goldilocks was a young girl with blond hair.

Originally, Goldilocks was an old woman with silver hair. The story ends with her breaking her neck trying to run away from the bears through the woods.

55.   In Beauty and the Beast, the Beast looked like a boar beast.
The beast was originally a three-headed winged snake demon.

56.   The Little Mermaid marries a prince and they live happily ever after.
The Prince marries another and the mermaid turns into foam.

57.   Pinocchio becomes a real boy and lives happily ever after.
Pinocchio beats Jiminy Cricket to death with a hammer and Pinocchio has his feet burned off, then hanged by villagers.
You know...for kids.

58.   Cinderella marries a prince and they live happily ever after.
In the Brother's Grimm version, Cinderella (known as Aschenputtel in this interpretation) gets a happy ending. I can't say the same about her evil stepsisters. In a desperate attempt to fit into the slipper, the stepsisters cut off their heels and toes to try and fit into the slipper.
To make it worse, in the middle of Aschenputtel's wedding, two doves appear FOR NO REASON and pluck out the stepsisters' eyes!

59.   In Snow White and the Seven Dwarves, the Evil witch dies by falling off a cliff.
The Evil Witch is forced to dance to death in boiling hot shoes.
That's why Walt Disney thought that this should be his first animated movie for children.

60.   Ratty is a rat character in The Wind in the Willows.
He is actually a vole (which are known as water rats.)

61.   In Gulliver's Travels, Gulliver went to Lilliput.
Gulliver's Travels was originally called Travels into Several Remote Nations of the World in Four Parts by Lemuel Gulliver, First a Surgeon, and then a Captain of Several Ships. Seriously.
Lilliput was Gulliver's first stop on his journey. He goes to Lilliput first where he meets a population of tiny people.
Then he goes to Brobdingnag, the land of giants.
Then he goes to Laputa, the floating island. Then he goes to Glubbdubdrib, where he meets the ghosts of historical figures. After that, he goes to some place called Japan.
His final destination is the Land of the Houyhnhnms, the land of talking horses before he ventures back home.

62. Superman first appears in Action Comics #1 published in June 1938.

Even the biggest Superman fans may not know this. Jerry Seigel created Superman in Reign of the Superman in 1933.

Superman was a bald, telekinetic villain with a purple costume and a gold cape. He resembled Superman's nemesis, Lex Luthor.

It's a different character with the same name, but technically it was Superman's first appearance.

63. Superman has always been able to fly at the speed of light.

In Action Comics #1 in 1938, Superman could jump one-eighth of a mile high. He could only run as fast as a speeding locomotive (which is pretty impressive but not as fast as light speed.)

Superman couldn't fly until years later.

64. Originally, Bruce Banner turned into a green Hulk when he got angry.

Bruce Banner used to turn into a grey Hulk at night-time. Grey was a color that aged badly in comics. It would deteriorate into a smudgy green. Marvel Comics made the Hulk turn green soon after.

65. Autographed comic books are worth a fortune.

If anyone writes on a comic book, including the original writer, its price will drastically go down.

Lou Ferringo (who played the Hulk in the tv show in the 1970s) met Stan Lee, the creator of Marvel Comics, Spiderman, the X-Men, and the Hulk. Lou asked Stan to sign his issue of The Incredible Hulk #1 which is worth about $125,000. But since Stan Lee wrote on it, it's not worth much now.

Many people ask comic book writers to autograph their comic books not realizing that they might be losing thousands (sometimes millions) of dollars.

66. In the story, Dr. Jekyll and Mr. Hyde, Mr. Hyde is a ten-foot hulking cannibalistic monster that kills dozens of people.

This idea has become popular thanks to the graphic novel and movie, The League of Extraordinary Gentlemen.

In the original story, Strange Case of Dr. Jekyll and Mr. Hyde (there's no "The" at the beginning of the title for some reason) by Robert Louis Stevenson, Mr. Hyde is four foot tall. He kills one person.

A four-foot "monster" doesn't work in Hollywood movies. But then again, neither did the League of Extraordinary Gentlemen. Terrible film. Give it a miss.

DINOSAURS

67.   **Dinosaurs were scaly.**
All dinosaurs had feathers. I have ruined Jurassic Park forever.

68.   **All dinosaurs lived together at the same time.**
Modern society is closer in time to the T-Rex than it is to the Stegosaurus by millions of years.

69.   **Velociraptors looked the same as they do in Jurassic Park.**
Velocirators were only a foot tall. Steven Spielberg liked their design and made them human-sized. In reality, they looked like an aggressive chicken.

70.   **Mammals evolved after the dinosaurs died out.**
Mammals lived before, during, and after the era of dinosaurs.

71.   **All reptiles in this period were dinosaurs.**
There were many giant lizard reptiles that lived during the Triassic, Cretaceous and Jurassic period that were not dinosaurs.

72.   **Dinosaurs lived in the sea.**
All dinosaurs lived on land. The most famous sea beast in the dinosauric era was the plesiosaurus (aka the Loch Ness monster) but it was a reptile as were many aquatic beasts at the time.

73.   **The biggest dinosaur ever was the Brachiosaurus.**
A dinosaur has only been recently discovered in Argentina called the Dreadnoughtus. It was the biggest dinosaur ever weighing 65 tons and measured 85 feet long.

74.   **The Brontosaurus was a long-necked dinosaur.**
Paleontologist O.C. Marsh discovered the first "Brontosaurus" skeleton in 1879. Since it didn't have a head, he used a skull of another dinosaur, the Camarasaurus and named the dinosaur the "Brontosaurus" (Thunder Lizard).

It turns out that the skeleton was actually of an Apatosaurus, a species that Marsh had discovered two years before. He tried to conceal this fact but it was eventually discovered.

So the Brontosaurus never existed. But if it did, it would've had feathers.

75.   There is a dinosaur that could shoot an ink-like substance at its prey.

Probably the scariest part of Jurassic Park involves a seemingly harmless dinosaur whose head seems to grow much like a peacock's tail to intimidate prey. It then shoots a gooey substance at one of the characters.

This dinosaur is called a dilophosaurus. It did exist but the goo and the sprouting mane were invented for the movie.

76.   Dinosaurs were savage beasts.

The majority of dinosaurs were herbivores and only ate plants.

77.   The Triceratops existed.

This is the dinosaur with two horns on top of its head and a rhino-like horn on its nose. It's probably the most identifiable dinosaur apart from the T-Rex and the Stegosaurus.

At least, it would be if it were real.

All Triceratops skeletons found are a teenage Torosaurus.

You might be thinking, "Stop ruining my childhood! What's next? Are you going to say the Tyrannosaurus Rex wasn't the most ferocious dinosaur ever?"

78.   The Tyrannosaurus Rex was the most ferocious dinosaur.

The T-Rex was one of the first identified dinosaurs so archeologists went nuts. It was unlike any other dinosaur identified at the time. It looked like the ultimate predator.

They have found fiercer dinosaurs since. The Gigantosaurus and the Acrocanthosaurus were bigger and fiercer versions of the Tyrannosaur. The T-Rex wasn't even that big. There were fifteen dinosaurs larger than the T-Rex. The Megaladon shark at the time was twice the size of the biggest Tyrannosaur.

The reason the T-Rex deserves its reputation is because it has the most powerful bite of any animal in history.

But it still had feathers.

79.   The T-Rexes could only see things when their prey was moving.

"Their vision is based off movement" is a great line in Jurassic Park but it's untrue. T-Rexes had exceptional eyesight.

80.   The fossils in museums are the original bones of the creatures.

Carbon dating is how archeologists calculate how old a fossil is. There is a compound in every living thing called carbon14. Understanding it can help scientists figure out how old fossils are.

About 50% of the carbon in an organism wears down every 5,568 years. So in another 5,568 years, there will only be 25% remaining and so on.

The dinosaurs went extinct at least 65 million years ago. Some of them went extinct 500 million years ago. So the chances of finding even a single bone intact from that period is slim. To find an entire skeleton from the Jurassic era is pretty much non-existent.

So when you see the skeleton of a Stegosaurus or Tricerato...I mean Torosaurus at museums, they are nearly always replicas.

81.   We know what dinosaurs looked like.

If one archeologist found a bone, and someone else found another bone thousands of miles away, and they studied the bones and discovered they came from the same dinosaur, they would have a better understanding of what it looked like. This can be the most frustrating jigsaw puzzle ever because some bones are just too small to survive millions of years. A lot of it is guesswork.

There are other factors that complicate this further. If every dinosaur had a trunk like an elephant, we wouldn't know. There are no bones in a trunk so there would be no evidence in the fossils to tell us this.

So what you see in museums is archeologists' best guess of what dinosaurs may have looked like. But. They. Had. Feathers.

82.   The first dinosaur ever discovered was a T-Rex.

The first dinosaur discovered was an Iguanodon (the dinosaur Godzilla is.) It was so called because people didn't know dinosaurs existed. Archeologists just thought it was a REALLY big iguana.

83.   Mankind will eventually clone a dinosaur.

Few things in science are impossible but cloning dinosaurs is one of them.

DNA has a half-life of 521 years. After that time, 50% of its chemical bonds will have withered away.

DNA would be unreadable after 1.5 million years and there would be nothing left of dinosaur DNA after 6.8 million years.

With the most recent dinosaurs dying out 65 million years ago, there is no theory as to how dinosaurs could ever come back to life.

DISORDERS

34.   Epileptics have seizures when exposed to flickering light.
One in twenty epileptics are photosensitive. Epileptics can have fits for numerous reasons such as stress, fatigue, or allergies.

35.   People with autism can do incredible mathematical problems like in the movie, Rain Man.
Only some autistic savants can do this but it is extremely rare.

36.   Twins attached to each other are called Siamese Twins.
Twins that are attached to each other are called Conjoined Twins. The first Conjoined twins on record were from Siam. They were known in the papers as Siamese Twins so people assumed that's what Conjoined Twins were called.

37.   Vertigo is a fear of heights.
Acrophobia is a fear of heights. There's a difference between a phobia and a condition. My father suffered from vertigo. He wasn't afraid of heights. He climbed the Great Wall of China. Twice.

But if he suddenly realized that he was near a cliff edge or building, his vertigo would start to affect him and he would suddenly feel like he was moving even though he was standing still.

You don't have to be high up to experience vertigo. People can suffer vertigo even when they are in the bottom story of a building.

38.   Lifting heavy objects can cause a hernia.
Lifting heavy objects is the easiest way to find out that you have a hernia. A hernia is when an organ has become misplaced. The most common understanding is when an organ like your intestine is mildly protruding into your abdomen which will cause intense pain.

Hernias occur when your body doesn't have enough collagen. Collagen is the protein the makes your skin and muscles flexible.

Collagen can break down due to genetics, age, or smoking.

39.   The most common illness doctors deal it with in the US is a cold.
Depression is the most common diagnosis in America. It's also the fourth most common diagnosis worldwide behind pneumonia, diarrhea, and AIDS.

About 3% of men suffer worldwide but for women, it could be two or three times more common.

90. Tourniquets should be applied to heavily bleeding wounds.

Tourniquets are banned in most countries, as cutting off circulation in any area of the body will exasperate the wound.

91. Giants are super strong.

One of the most famous giants was Andre Roussimoff who was better known as the wrestler, Andre the Giant, standing 7ft 4.

Andre starred in the movie The Princess Bride. There's a scene where he catches a young girl. When he's holding her, she looks like a toddler because of his size. But the filmmakers had to make a support under Andre's arms because he couldn't hold her without experiencing excruciating pain. Andre was so weak in his later life, he could be knocked off his feet with a push from a child.

Most giants' bones grow so fast, they don't have a chance to calcify and harden. This makes their bones brittle, so they experience daily agony.

92. Steroids cause extreme anger known as 'Roid Rage.

If you were naturally content person who didn't experience intense stress and you were given steroids, it's incredibly unlikely you would experience aggressive side effects.

So why does 'Roid Rage happen? 7% of people are clinically repressed. This means that 7% of people are almost incapable of expressing certain emotions. Steroids will over-stimulate your emotions, which means that people who take this drug may experience intense anger or even panic or depression.

But this doesn't mean that there's a 7% chance of 'Roid Rage happening. If you feel like you need to take steroids, it's likely you feel insecure and you are suffering from clinical repression, which is probably undiagnosed.

If you gave a hundred random people anabolic steroids, about seven of them would experience side effects. But because repressed people tend to be attracted to anabolic steroids, 20% of steroid-users statistically will experience side effects with their mood.

93. The best way to deal with anger is to vent.

This works for most emotions. When you cry, you feel better afterward. But when you lash out in anger, you feel better because anger temporarily makes you feel more powerful.

But it's addictive. The angrier you get, the more anger you want to unleash. It works in an unhelpful and vicious cycle.

94.   Scurvy is an ancient disease that pirates suffered.
You can still get scurvy if you lack Vitamin C. This is rare because food is so accessible in modern society. But it's not uncommon in newborn babies or the elderly who are ill and malnourished.

95.   Attention Hyperactive Deficit Disorder (ADHD) is common.
Just because a person is a bit hyper or seems to have poor concentration doesn't mean they suffer ADHD. I know two people who had ADHD. Both of them required medication like Ritalin for six months to calm down but they suffered severe side effects for years like depression and night terrors. A specialist needs to diagnose you. You can't just diagnose yourself. There are many disorders people feel compelled to diagnose themselves with such as...

96.   Night terrors are common.
Some people claim to have night terrors when they have a really bad nightmare. We've all had nightmares so bad we couldn't get back to sleep.

Night terrors are much worse than that. Night terrors only tend to happen as part of Post Traumatic Stress Syndrome, mental illness or side effects from medication. You can't get them just from stress or anxiety. After a night terror, you physically couldn't function the next day. You wouldn't be able to go to work or school afterwards.

When a nightmare is over, you recognize that it was just a dream. A night terror is so intense, you can't recognize the danger is over and it is not uncommon for the person to run out of the house, attack people, hysterically screaming, crying, and hyperventilating.

About 10% of people claimed to have suffered night terrors but it is more like 1% at most.

97.   Insomnia is common.
Most people who believe they have insomnia simply have an imbalanced sleep pattern. Insomnia is an inability to sleep.

People with a bad sleep pattern do sleep about six hours a day but it's spread unevenly throughout the day.

Insomniacs sleep for only two to four hours every day.
Insomnia can only be corrected with therapy and medication.

98.   Dyslexia is common.
Some people believe they have dyslexia when they simply haven't read much. Dyslexia is a neurological disorder and it has nothing to do with how often a person reads.

FOOD AND DRINK

99. **French fries are from France.**
They're Belgian. Frenching means to cut into thin strips.

100. **Croissants come from France.**
France loses this one too. Croissants are Austrian.

101. **Champagne is French.**
Champagne originates from England in 1662. It was nowhere near as nice as the French who perfected it two centuries later, but in essence, it was still champagne.

102. **Spaghetti is Italian.**
Spaghetti is Chinese (and I don't mean noodles.) Spaghetti the way Westerners think of it hails from China. Magellan tasted it on his travels to Asia and brought it back to Venice where it became popular with Italians.

103. **Apples are from America.**
Apples originate from Kazakhstan.

104. **Bobbing for apples originated in America.**
The Romans created apple bobbing.

105. **Brazil nuts are nuts.**
Brazil nuts are seeds.

106. **Cashew nuts are nuts.**
Cashew nuts are sprouts.

107. **Coconuts are nuts.**
Coconuts are drupes.

108. **Peanuts are nuts.**
Peanuts are beans.

109. **Walnuts are nuts.**
Walnuts are ....fruit? Are we even TRYING to name food anymore!???
Why don't we just call coffee a fruit!?!?!

110.   Coffee is made from beans.
Coffee are seeds....which means that coffee is technically a fruit. Coffee actually grows on trees just like bananas. Oh wait...

111.   Bananas grow on trees.
Banana trees don't exist (which makes Donkey Kong terribly inaccurate.) Bananas are berries that grow from a banana seed from the ground. Speaking of berries...

112.   Strawberries are berries.
Strawberries are an aggregate accessory fruit.

113.   Raspberries are berries.
Raspberries are perennial fruit.

114.   Blackberries are berries.
Blackberries are bramble fruit, not berries. But watermelons, pineapples, and avocados are berries. Never ask why.

115.   Japanese eat sushi all of the time.
The sushi we eat doesn't look or taste the same as Japanese sushi. The sushi we eat is a Western concoction attempting to emulate Japanese food.
Most Japanese people eat sushi a few times a year.

116.   Decaffeinated coffee has no caffeine.
Decaf still has 3% caffeine.

117.   Coca-Cola was originally green.
Even the Coca-Cola website states "Coke has always been brown in color, since its start." Only the bottles were originally green.

118.   Coca-Cola created Santa Claus.
The first version of Santa goes back thousands of years in Norse mythology. He was called Odin. Anthony Hopkins played him in the movie, Thor. He was a magical man that gave gifts to children and he flew on Sleipnir, his eight-legged horse (which is where the idea of a magical reindeer comes from.)
But surely Coca-Cola invented the modern depiction of Santa, right?
Coca-Cola was created in 1886. They started using Santa as a marketing tool in 1931. But the drawings of St. Nick depicted the way we know him have been on magazine covers since 1908.

119. **Only two Coca-Cola executives know the Coke's formula and they only know half of it each.**

The Coca-Cola ingredients are accessible on the Internet. But one of the ingredients is de-cocainized flavored coca leaves. You can't get this anywhere except through connections of the highest order at Coca-Cola. Even if you could get it and you could start your own "brand of Coke," how would that work?

If you just rip off Coke, you will be sued. If you created a new brand, everyone would see it as a cheap knock-off. Coca-Cola knew that when they lost millions trying to sell New Coke. If Coca-Cola couldn't sell a different Coke, what chance would you have?

120. **If you leave a tooth in Coca-Cola overnight, it will dissolve.**

Coke will not dissolve a tooth in a day. Teeth will dissolve after a long time in Coke but that's what phosphoric acid and citric acid do. The same thing would happen if you put a tooth in orange juice.

121. **Don't drink alcohol or caffeinated drinks when dehydrated, as you will lose more water in the long run.**

If you were in a desperate situation like in a desert or lost at sea, you should drink water to hydrate yourself. There are some drinks you are meant to avoid as they supposedly hydrate you a little then dehydrate you a lot like tea, coffee, coke or alcohol.

But it isn't true. Water will hydrate you the most efficiently but the other drinks will not cause dehydration.

Any drink will hydrate you except seawater.

122. **Honey has an expiry date of a few years.**

Honey can last for over 32,000 years.

In an apocalypse, forget about canned food; go for honey.

HISTORY

123. **The Egyptian Pyramids looked the same now as they did when they were built.**

When the Pyramids were built, they were covered in white gold that would glow at night. This covered the interior that we see today. In Ancient Egypt, the Pyramids were smooth, not blocky.

But weather and thieves have eradicated all of the white gold throughout millennia. The apex capstone at the top of the Great Pyramid of Giza is still barely intact so you can see how the pyramids should've looked back in their day.

124.   Pharaohs were seen as Gods.
The Egyptians knew Khufu was not divine. The Romans made this assumption because they saw the Egyptians bow to Prince Khufu. Romans found it disrespectful to bow to kings because they believed the only person worth bowing to was a God.

125.   When Tutankhamen's tomb was unearthed, The Mummy's Curse killed all of the archeologists.
The inscription, "They who enter this sacred tomb shall swift be visited by wings of death" never existed. That was in the movie. The mummy didn't come back to life either, just to let you know.

But the archeologists died, right? Yes. Caranarvon did die shortly after the tomb was opened but he was very ill before he went to Egypt.

You may have heard of a security guard that died who guarded King Tut in the museum. That is true. He did die....fifty years later. So either the curse is nonsense or that mummy is taking his sweet time exacting his revenge.

126.   Tutankhamen was an important pharaoh.
King Tut didn't do anything of significance in his time compared to other pharaohs like Ramses and Khufu. So why is he remembered?

For decades, historians hoped to discover rooms full of historical wonders in Ancient Egypt. Instead, they kept finding abandoned tombs. Thieves had stolen money, gold, jewels, and documents that would give modern man a look into how the Ancient Egyptians lived. King Tut is the only Pharaonic tomb that was untouched by thieves.

When the Missing Link was found in 2008 (Australopithecus aka Lucy,) it is significant because we found it. But that doesn't mean Lucy was significant in her time. King Tut is significant out of circumstance, not achievement.

That is why he's the most famous Egyptian apart from Cleopatra. Oh wait...

127.   Cleopatra was Egyptian.
Cleopatra VII was Greek. Cleopatra was a direct ancestor of Ptolemy, a teacher to Alexander the Great.

128.   Cleopatra was beautiful.
Cleopatra's image is on Roman currency. The word "flattering" doesn't spring to mind. She had a big nose, a thick chin, thin lips (and very good marketing.)

129.   Cleopatra witnessed the pyramids being built.
The pyramids were finished in 2540 BC. Cleopatra died over two millennia later in 30 BC. This means that Cleopatra is closer to our time than the construction of the pyramids.

130.   Slaves built the pyramids.
A pharaoh would never trust slaves to build a tomb in his honor. Highly skilled craftsmen built the pyramids.

131.   Vikings had horned helmets.
Many Viking helmets can be seen in museums. None of them have horns. They would be totally impractical in battle.

132.   Vikings were wild, ruthless, savages.
Vikings were so particular about their appearance that each Viking had a delicate grooming kit with tiny scissors, razors, ear spoons, and tweezers to keep their beard and hair perfectly groomed.
You might think, "Nonsense! Where would they keep this kit when they were invading towns?"
In their purse. Let me say that again. Vikings. Wore. Purses. During battle. Male Vikings. On purpose.
Also, it was the Viking women had far more power than men. It was they who chose who to marry and when to divorce.
Most Vikings bleached their hair with soap to make it blonde.
If you think I have ruined your image of Vikings, guess who's next?

133.   Gladiators in the Coliseum were extremely well-built.
Gladiators were fat. Really fat.
Gladiators were similar to pro-wrestling but not in the way you'd think. Wrestling nowadays like the WWE is a show business. Popular wrestlers make people buy tickets. You can't be popular if you're dead. If the audience liked certain gladiators and the fighters put up a good fight, neither fighter would have to be put to death.
But why were they fat? People paid for the Coliseum to see one thing – blood. The bigger a person is, the more blood he can spill.
Wrestlers in the entertainment business do a technique called "blading." This means they will cut themselves in a spot that spills a lot of blood but it isn't dangerous.
Gladiators knew how to spill a lot of blood without hitting vital organs. Once enough blood was spilled, the audience was content, even without a death. The fatter you were, the longer you would live for (in the Coliseum, not real life.)

134. **In the Coliseum, a thumbs-down from the Emperor meant "death."**

A thumbs-up symbolized a death sentence where a fist meant that the fighter would be spared.

135. **Christians were thrown to the lions in the Coliseum.**

Emperor Nero persecuted Christians before the Coliseum was even built. By the time it was constructed; the majority of Romans were Christians.

136. **In the time that the movie Gladiator was based, Commodus stole the throne when he killed Maximus's father, who was the Emperor.**

It was Maximus who usurped the throne in 383 A.D. not Commodus.

Maximus and Commodus had no personal relationship as they lived two centuries apart.

Commodus wasn't an evil emperor and he didn't die in battle but anticlimactically in the bathtub.

137. **The Dark Ages was the worst time in mankind's history, especially in science and technology.**

People believe that the Dark Ages ended as soon as the Renaissance began.

But this was the time when Islam spread astronomy, physics, literature, architecture, medicine, philosophy, and mathematics. Muslims, or follower of Islam)spread their advancements in schools, libraries, and created the most detailed social welfare ever at the time.

This was considered The Middle East Golden Age. If this had spread to Europe, the Renaissance might never have happened nor needed to.

138. **Pirates were savage, evil men.**

Pirates accepted everyone no matter their religious belief, gender, race or sexual orientation. Pirates practiced democracy and health insurance.

They accepted gay marriage and weddings were common onboard.

They still attacked and plundered people; they just had standards. Kinda.

139.   Pirates had pet parrots.
Pirates didn't have pets. Of a crew of dozens, travelling hundreds of miles through violent storms where the chances of crewmembers dying from starvation or disease being very likely, the last thing a pirate would do is bring on another mouth to feed.

140.   Pirates talked like pirates.
Pirates talked the same way as everybody else. The "pirate voice" was popularized by the 1950s Disney movie, Treasure Island.

141.   Pirates had peg-legs.
There is one record of a pirate with a peg leg. His name is unknown.

142.   Pirates made people walk the plank.
There is one record of this ever occurring.
The ship had to be constantly cleaned to prevent the possibility of disease and infection. So pirates needed all the people they could get and wouldn't find new ways to kill their own crew.

143.   Pirates buried treasure.
William McKidd is the only pirate that has been recorded as burying treasure.

144.   The Skull and Crossbones symbol originated from pirates.
The Spanish originally used this symbol to label cemeteries.

145.   Blackbeard was the most powerful pirate of all.
Edward "Blackbeard" Teach was an infamous pirate. But there is one pirate far greater; a Chinese ex-prostitute called Ching Shih. Her husband was a pirate captain. When he died, she was left with all of his crew. Over time, she became the most powerful pirate ever commanding 1,800 vessels and 80,000 pirates.
(Why doesn't she get a movie? Maybe Johnny Depp could play her too.)

146.   People believed the world was flat before Columbus discovered America.
An Ancient Greek mathematician, Eratosthenes deduced that the Earth was round in 500 B.C.
He perfectly calculated the circumference of the Earth over a millennium before it was confirmed because why the hell not. He had some spare time one weekend and invented geography.

147. **Christopher Columbus thought the world was round when everyone else thought it was flat.**
Columbus thought the Earth was pear-shaped.
The idea of a flat Earth has never been a popular theory.

148. **Christopher Columbus discovered America.**
Bjarni Herjolfsson of Iceland was the first to find America 500 years before Columbus. Did Columbus do anything?!

149. **Christopher Columbus landed in America.**
Columbus couldn't have discovered America because he never landed in it. He landed in the Bahamas and ventured from Dominica all the way southward. He never went to the area that became the United States in his entire life.

150. **Wigwams were pointy tents that Native Americans lived in.**
When you picture a Native American's tent, that is a teepee.
Wigwams looked like big, shaggy, round houses. Some Native American tribes lived in homes like this at the time of Columbus.

151. **Native Americans were killed because settlers gave them quilts infected with smallpox.**
Up to 100 million Native Americans died just before the settlers arrived from a plague that dwarfs the Black Death.
The Black Death killed 60% of Europe. This plague killed 96% of both North and South America. Settlers said countless towns didn't have a single person alive because of the plague.
But if there wasn't a plague, surely the settlers would've beaten the Native Americans, right? Because everyone knows the natives were peaceful, right?

152. **Native Americans were peaceful.**
When I was told in school that Vikings discovered America before Columbus, I was surprised no one ever asked, "Why didn't they take over?" Vikings were ruthless savages, right? (Read Fact 132 to remind yourself why that's not true.)
The Vikings fled America (that's right, they ran away) because the Native Americans could throw spears with such force, that it would pierce the Vikings armor and kill them. That's not a bow and arrow. A human arm could hurl a spear that penetrated metal! That's like the power of every Avenger combined.
So if they had all of their tribes ready for battle when the Settlers arrived, America would never have been conquered.

THE HUMAN BODY

153. Human beings have five senses.

It's debatable how many sense we have but it's at least ten. There are the five obvious ones – Taste, touch, smell, sight, hearing. Then we get to the more obscure ones.

Equlibrioception – sense of balance

Thermoception – sense of temperature

Proprioception – body awareness

Nociception – sense of pain

Chronoception – sense of time

There's a lot more "mini-senses" but for the sake of keeping it simple, we still say there are five "official" senses.

154. Human beings have a tongue map and certain sections react to sour, bitter, sweet, etc.

You do have a tongue map but it's not as even as what is taught in biology class. It is far more sporadic. A doctor couldn't point to a part of your tongue and tell you which taste it experiences.

155. If a finger or toe ever gets chopped off, put it on ice so it can be re-attached later.

Ice deadens the nerves preventing any chance of re-attaching the digit.

Ideally, an unattached digit should be put in a reasonably cool and germ-free container but not in anything freezing.

156. You need eight glasses of water a day.

You need the equivalent of eight glasses of water a day. So if you have this much water a day and then you eat a watermelon, you are going to feel bloated. The "eight glasses" includes water in the food you eat.

157. Don't ever wake a sleepwalker.

If you wake up someone while they sleep, they will be just as disorientated as anybody who is suddenly awoken. If a sleepwalker were about to step on something hazardous, why wouldn't you wake them? That's just mean.

158. When you are pregnant, you can't conceive another child.

It's very rare but has been documented several times in humans. It is known as superfetation.

159. **Liars tell stories that don't add up and have huge gaps of information missing.**

If you were asked what movie did you see at the cinema three months ago, you would need a moment to recall (and you mightn't be able to.)

If you pretended you went to the cinema three months ago because you were doing something illegal, you would have your lie prepared in an attempt to cover your tracks.

Truth-tellers don't remember trivial information like a specific day you went to see a movie. But liars can call upon their lies instantly because they don't want to get caught.

160. **Liars avoid eye contact.**

This is the most common stereotype for liars, which means it is the first characteristic people try to identify when accusing someone of lying.

However, since everybody knows this concept, it is more likely that a liar will maintain eye contact to give the impression that he or she is telling the truth.

A liar hopes to be believed. A person telling the truth expects to be believed. So liars will try harder to convince a person they are telling a truth than someone who actually is.

161. **Liars touch their face or overuse hand gestures.**

Some people are simply prone to scratching themselves or over gesticulating. If you think somebody is lying to you, you shouldn't focus on what they do but what they say. You can fake a lot of facial expressions to seem genuine but it's incredibly tough for your voice to sound sincere when you aren't.

It's far easier to tell if someone is lying on the phone than in person because you may focus on the wrong things.

162. **If someone gets angry when they are accused of lying, they are lying.**

A liar wants to come across that they are telling the truth and is more likely to stay calm. Getting angry will make it harder for a liar to maintain their lies and keep their story straight.

Nobody likes being accused of something they haven't done so it's far more likely than someone telling the truth will react to an accusation with anger.

163.   You need to be super strong to rip a phone book in half.
This is a trick. Get a good grip on the spine and then bend it sharply so it breaks. Immediately pull the two pieces in different directions; left hand forward and right hand back and it tears easily. It has nothing to do with strength. Even a child can do it.

164.   If you swallow gum, it will take seven years to digest.
Surely if this was true, it would block the rest of your food (unless the gum traffics other food and that's just silly.)

165.   The inside of the body looks like the diagrams you have seen in biology.
That picture has been simplified so you can see every body part. In most diagrams, every organ seems neat and they fit together like a jigsaw. But you can't show an accurate depiction of your organs on a flat 2D picture.

For example, in diagrams your lungs look like they take up the top half of your upper body in diagrams. Your lungs fill almost your entire upper body. The lungs start at your collarbone and end below your belly button.

Diagrams make your liver look like it's the size of a grapefruit when it is nearly the width of your waist.

If you want to have a good understanding of what the inside of your body looks like, look at 3D videos online, not 2D pictures.

166.   Human beings should sleep for eight hours a day.
Human beings haven't evolved to sleep longer than a few hours. For millennia, there was no set time. People didn't have clocks or watches. Only in the last hundred years did we have a time that we all agreed on.

Our ancestors went to sleep when it got dark and awoke when they thought it was time to get up.

Our ancestors may not have had shelter and they could be mauled to death by a wild animal at any moment. As a result, we have never been inclined to sleep longer than a few hours here and there rather than the set-in-stone times we are used to today.

This is why people wake up an average of nine times every night. You won't remember most of these times but it happens to everyone.

If you want a definitive answer, seven hours is recommended to re-energize your body.

167. If you haven't slept in a while, you should sleep-in the next day.

Your body doesn't work that way. That's like refueling a car beyond maximum capacity. If a car is designed to take a certain amount of fuel, you can't force it to have more and expect it to work better. If the human body is supposed to sleep for seven or eight hours, it's not going to work better because you slept for twelve hours. People are less alert when they sleep too much rather than sleep too little.

168. Women have a higher resistance to pain than men.

Women have half the pain tolerance of men because they have twice as many pain receptors.

When our male ancestors were hunting and gathering, the men would have to fight predators, prey, and rivals. If men registered the same amount of pain as a woman does during battle, a male's body would tell them to quit or run.

Women need to have more pain receptors so they can sense if anything is wrong when they are pregnant. This is where the idea of women's intuition comes from. A man will not be able to register the level of pain or feeling as delicately as a woman.

Women live longer than men. It's not because they are less inclined in getting cancer. They're just better at detecting if something is wrong because their sensors are more receptive than men.

169. We use 10% of our brains.

Everyone has seen a diagram of the brain with arrows that point at sections that say "Sight" "Taste" "Smell" and so on. Have you ever seen a diagram where all of these captions were just pointing at 10% of the brain and the rest of it was blank?

We can only use 10% of our brain at one time. We know this because the more we multi-task, the more our attention to each individual task starts to fade. Your brain can do many things but it can't do them simultaneously.

170. The brain is pink.

The brain's pinkness comes from the blood cells. When you die, the brain's color turns to grey.

171. The brain is brain-shaped.

The brain is shaped the way it is because it is in the head. Once it is taken out of the body, it will then become a shapeless, gooey blob unless it is preserved.

172.   You can be a left-brained kind of person.
If you are creative, that doesn't mean that you are mainly using the left side of your brain. Creativity can be divided into many categories and all of these sections are distributed randomly around your brain.

173.   The bigger your brain is, the smarter you are.
The sperm whale has the biggest brain weighing eighteen pounds. That's six times more than a human.
So why aren't they flying in spaceships and colonizing Mars? How "smart" you are has to do with the ratio of brain to body weight. However…

174.   Human beings have the largest brain proportioned to their body weight.
The ant's brain makes up 6% of its entire weight, triple the proportion of a human brain. But insects can't have complex neurons like the way we do. Humans have 40,000 times as many neurons as ants. This allows us to develop intellect and self-awareness.
Ants are excellent at surviving and have been on Earth 26 million times longer than humans. But they probably couldn't split an atom or unlock an iPhone.

175.   When you breathe in, you should suck your gut in. When you breathe out, you should stick your gut out.
You're meant to do the opposite. It might take a few days to stop this habit considering you've been doing it most of your life. It will help your breathing, your projection, and even your stamina.

176.   If a person flat-lines, you need to use defibrillator paddles (the ones where doctors shout, "CLEAR" and shock your heart.)
Defibrillators do nothing to an unresponsive heart. You need to use CPR chest compressions. Defibrillators are used for arrhythmia.

INVENTIONS

177.   The calculator was invented a few decades ago.
Blaise Pascal invented his Pascaline calculator in 1640, almost 500 years ago.
If you think that's incredible, you will be pretty desensitized by the end of this chapter when you realize just how old all of our "recent inventions" are.

178. Henry Ford invented the assembly line.

Ford popularized the idea of one person being responsible for one simple job. With this technique, his workers could build cars much faster than building them from scratch.

But the assembly line was invented by the Chinese to create the Terracotta Army. At least Henry Ford invented the automobile, right?

179. Henry Ford invented the automobile.

Nicolas-Joseph Cugnot invented the horseless carriage (it looked like a barrel with wheels) in 1771, over a century before Ford's Quadricycle.

But Cugnot's automobile crashed after one drive. Ford's Model T automobile became popular once the assembly line strategy (that he didn't invent) helped mass produce them.

180. Steve Jobs invented the iPod.

Although Apple invented the iPod as we know it, Kane Kramer created the first portable digital media player in1979. He needed to raise $90,000 but he couldn't do it in time before his patent expired.

181. James Watt invented the Engine.

Hero of Alexandria invented the first steam engine back in 331 B.C. two millennia before James Watt. It was used to rotate a globe on its axis.

182. Vending machines are a recent invention.

Hero also invented vending machines (he had a lot of time on his hands.) They could only supply one thing –holy water.

183. Automatic doors were created in the last century.

Hero's only hobby seems to be inventing things because he invented the automatic doors too.

184. The railway was invented about two centuries ago.

An unknown inventor invented the railway in 600 B.C. in Greece in Corinth. But so what? There were no steam engines back then so it was useless.

Oh wait. You just read in Fact 181 that Hero invented steam engines 300 hundreds later after the railway.

But nobody thought of putting the two together. If they did, we would have had trains nearly 2,500 years early!

185.   Thomas Edison invented the light bulb.
Humphrey Davy was the inventor of the light bulb.
Frederick de Moleyn patented it.
Many inventions go through a lot of prototypes that rarely resemble the finished product. So you would assume that Edison must've invented the light bulb that we know of today.
But Joseph Swan invented the modernized bulb.
So why does Edison get the credit?
Because he was a bully. He didn't even know how to use electricity efficiently.
His competitor, Nikola Tesla used alternating currents (AC.)
AC is far more efficient than Edison's direct current (DC.) Edison only succeeded because he threatened and mocked his competitors.
If we used AC from the beginning instead of DC, our technology would be at least 50 years more advanced than it is now.

186.   Thomas Edison invented the X-Ray.
Wilhelm Rontgen invented the X-Ray in 1895. Once again, Edison insisted his version was the most efficient X-Ray using bullying tactics.

187.   Thomas Edison invented the sound recorder.
Edouard Martinville invented the very first phonograph in 1860, seventeen years before Edison.
Wait...what did Edison invent again?

188.   Thomas Edison invented the microphone.
At this point, Edison is shaping up to be a charlatan because Emile Berliner invented the microphone in 1879.
Alexander Graham Bell believed Berliner was so superior to Edison's, he bought the patent for it to use when he invented the telephone....
Wait a minute....

189.   Alexander Graham Bell invented the telephone.
Antonio Meucci was the first to create a working telephone while Bell was still tweaking his version. But once Bell realized that Meucci was going to beat him to it, he ran to the patent office and got a patent for his "invention" hours before Meucci. Wow, inventors were really bad sore losers, weren't they?

90.   Edward Jenner invented inoculations in 1798 when he created a vaccine against smallpox.

3,000 years ago, a Hindu physician Dhanwantari used to infect his patients with small traces of a disease to prove they build a tolerance to the real one.

Okay, Dhanwantari may have invented the inoculation before Jenner, but Jenner created a vaccine against smallpox, right?

So what prehistoric disease did Dhanwantari vaccinate against? Smallpox.

Dhanwantari's vaccines weren't as good as Jenner's, but he made patients with pox thirty times more likely to live.

So how come nobody adopted his techniques?

Because it was disgusting! If you had smallpox now (somehow) and the doctor said the only cure was pouring cow pus into your blood, would you do it? I wouldn't blame you if you said no. You would probably die, but I still wouldn't blame you.

91.   Bill Gates invented the Internet and the World Wide Web.

Firstly, the Internet and the World Wide Web are not the same thing. The Internet is a network of info connecting all computers globally. The worldwide web (www) is a means to access that information. Bill Gates invented neither.

Tim Berners-Lee and Robert Cailliau created the World Wide Web in 1990.

No single person invented the Internet. Many people from 1961 to 1983 helped forge the Net. If I had to credit one man, Larry Roberts created the first functioning long-distance computer in 1965.

92.   The Wright Brothers were the first people to fly a plane.

Gustav Whitehead was the first pilot. He flew two separate flights (just to show off) before Orville and Wilbur Wright. There are claims of earlier flights by other aviators but no irrefutable proof. Reporters saw Gustav's flight in 1902 so there is no question he beat the Wright Brothers to it.

So how come the Wrights Brothers became famous instead? Because they took photos.

93.   Thomas Crapper invented the toilet.

Oh come on! He must have invented it! His name is Crapper for crying out loud!

He modified the toilet but it was invented thousand years ago in China. Toilet paper was invented a few decades later. Not sure why nobody got on that sooner.

194.   The first invention to break the sound barrier was the fighter jet.

The whip broke the sound barrier 7,000 years ago in China. The snapping sound a whip makes is a sonic boom.

195.   Landmines were invented in World War 1.

In the twelfth century, the Chinese would bury a box of gunpowder, oil and iron pellets. It is primitive compared to today's landmines but in essence, it worked the same.

196.   Crossbows were invented in medieval times.

The Chinese invented crossbows in 400 B.C. (At this point, just assume the answer is always The Chinese.)

As you can tell in this chapter, a lot of the "actual first" inventions were a more simplified version of what we know today. But Chinese crossbows were better in some ways than crossbows of today. They could fire ten bolts in fifteen seconds and each bolt was a guaranteed kill because each bolt was dipped in poison.

Crossbows also have the world record for being the longest commonly used mechanical device in history.

197.   Chinese Checkers was invented in China.

Chinese Checkers was invented in Germany in 1892. Why is the ONE THING that's not from China called Chinese Checkers?

198.   Chinese fortune cookies come from China.

They come from California, USA (which you would've known if you saw Iron Man 3. It's a very educational film.)

199.   Shopping malls are a recent invention.

The Ancient Romans had shopping malls over 2,000 years ago. It was called Trajan's market and was in the center of Ancient Rome. What is most bizarre is that it is still standing today.

200.   Robots were invented a few decades ago.

The first robot was created in 400 BC.

If that blows your mind, relax. It's not Terminator standard or anything.

The inventor was Archytas of Ancient Greece. His automaton resembled a pigeon and would compress steam inside itself to fly. It didn't just fly a few feet. It flew 300 meters before it ran out of steam (literally.) He did this to understand how animals fly and accidentally created the first functioning robot ever.

01. Alarm clocks were invented about a century ago.
Alarm clocks were also invented in Ancient Greece in 400 B.C.
The "clock" looked like four hourglasses attached to each other.
The top one was filled with water and slowly filtered to the one below.
When it got to the third vessel, the forced air would produce a whistling noise waking the person up.
The final vessel collected the water so it could be used again.

02. Flamethrowers were invented during World War 1.
Flamethrowers were invented in Ancient Greece. Again. For the third time in a row. An unknown Greek engineer invented it in 672 A.D. It was called Greek Fire and was used to burn down rival ships at sea.

03. Central heating is a recent invention.
Many people believe it was the Ancient Romans who invented central heating but it was....the Greeks??? Seriously? Is there an invention those guys didn't make?
Greek central heating consisted of pipes tunneled under the floors of homes that pumped warm water during the winter.

04. Plumbing has existed for a few centuries.
Plumbing existed in 2700 B.C. in Greek, Roman, Persian, Indian, and Chinese civilizations.
It wasn't until the nineteenth century where plumbing standards dramatically improved. They used lead for the pipes hence the name plumbing (Latin for lead.)

05. Doorknobs have existed for centuries.
You can see that many inventions were invented millennia earlier than you assumed. But what about inventions that are more recent than you expected?
There are countless historical movies that have doorknobs. But Osbourn Dorsey (he had "door" in his name?) invented the doorknob as recently as 1878. That was after Abraham Lincoln was president. Yet if you watch the movie Lincoln, you will see deceitful doorknobs all over the place.
In fact, if you watch any movies based in 1500s, 1600s, 1700s, or early 1800s and there are doorknobs everywhere!

MISCELLANEOUS

206. You have used tinfoil.
If you have told someone you have used tinfoil, congratulations because you are a liar. Tinfoil added a weird taste to whatever it wrapped around and was replaced by aluminum foil in 1910.

207. Recycling is cheap and creates less pollution and exerts less energy.
Different elements recycle differently. So the process of recycling one material can be cheaper but can cause pollution.
Recycling a different material might cause no pollution but it is more expensive than starting from scratch.
A lot of items rarely recycle back into their original form.
The only material that works the way people think ALL recycling works is with aluminum cans. Aluminum cans cause no pollution to be recycled and it is cheaper to re-use it than to make another one from scratch.
So recycling works, but it may not be as effective as you would imagine.

208. A gargoyle is a beast-like statue.
That's called a grotesque. A gargoyle is a statue that spews water from its mouth. Its name is derived from the word "gargle."

209. Diamonds are rare.
You could give everyone on Earth a cupful of diamonds.

210. Diamond is the hardest substance in the world.
Diamond is the seventh hardest substance (but it is the hardest natural substance.) Scientists have created six substances harder including graphene, the world's hardest substance. Mineral hardness is measured on the Mohs Scale of 1 to 10. When this scale was created, diamond was the hardest substance measuring 10. By comparison, talcum powder is 1, chalk is 2, and quartz is 7.
But graphene is 15.8 on the Mohs scale!! It literally broke the scale! It is over one and a half times harder than the hardest natural mineral on Earth.

211. Diamonds come from coal.
Diamonds are billions of years old. Diamonds are older than plants, which means they have to be older than coal.

212.   Trigonometry was created to benefit mathematics.

Trigonometry wasn't taken seriously as a vital part of mathematics until Muslims realized they could use it to understand where they needed to turn to face Mecca during prayer.

Seriously. They used trigonometry to pray to God.

213.   Algebra was created to benefit mathematics.

Like trigonometry, algebra was not taken seriously for a long time until it was discovered that it could be used to simplify convoluted inheritance laws in Islam.

Teenagers complain that algebra and trigonometry are pointless, but once again, Muslims finds a way to use it practically.

214.   Your schoolteachers used to write on the blackboard with chalk.

Your schoolteachers used gypsum to write on the blackboard. Chalk has never been used for this purpose.

Gypsum and chalk look identical but are composed of different materials.

Gypsum comes from the Greek word "gypsos" which means....chalk...but it's still not chalk.

215.   Stockbroking is the profession with the most drug users.

Nope. It's not athletes, artists, musicians, or actors either. It's not even drug-dealers.

The most common drug users are restaurant workers and construction workers.

216.   The toilet is the dirtiest place in your house.

The following places have more germs, dirt, and bacteria than your toilet –

a) Your cutting board has twice as much.
b) Your keyboard has five times as much.
c) Your phone has 500 times as much.
d) Your carpet has 4,000 times as much.
e) Your kitchen sponge has 200,000 times more germs than your toilet.

Sponge...you win.

MOVIES

217. **Movies were made for our entertainment.**
Movies were made on a bet. Eadweard Muybridge believed that a horse's legs are all off the ground at some point in mid-gallop but his friend Leland Stanford disagreed.

Eadweard decided to take lots of shots of a horse running and he compiled the shots together to form the first moving picture in 1878. It is now known as A Horse in Motion.

But he only did it to win money. Which he did.

218. **Waterworld is the most unsuccessful movie of all time losing $100 million.**
Waterworld didn't lose money. It wasn't a success because a movie needs to make twice as much as it cost to make to be considered a profit.

Waterworld cost $175 million, which means it needs to make $350 million to be considered a profit. It only made $264 million, which is where the idea of losing nearly $100 million comes from.

The most unsuccessful film is The Adventures of Pluto Nash, which lost $93 million. If you haven't heard of it...that is my point.

219. **Godzilla's famous roar is from a wild animal.**
Most movie monsters sounds are from animals. King Kong's roar is an edited lion roar and Jurassic Park's T-Rex roar is from the ferocious....walrus... huh...

Godzilla has the most iconic roar. Strangely, it isn't from an animal. Akira Ifukube came up with the idea for the sound by stroking a violin chord with a leather glove. I don't know if Akira has waaaaay too much time on his hands or if he is a genius.

220. **The original Frankenstein starred Boris Karloff in 1931.**
There is a sixteen-minute Frankenstein film made in 1910. It is more like a staged play but it was filmed so it counts. The Monster looks much hairier and has none of the distinctive attributes we use to identify the Monster. The bizarre thing is that the producer was none other than the duplicitous Thomas Edison!

221. **Frankenstein's assistant in the movie is called Igor.**
Frankenstein's assistant is called Fritz. Igor was a hunchback character in the second sequel Son of Frankenstein.

222. **The most expensive movie ever is Titanic.**

In this day and age, a movie that cost more than Titanic comes out almost every month.

Many people would say the most expensive movie would be Superman Returns, King Kong, or Avatar as they all cost over $250 million. If you think you're clever, you might say it's Cleopatra in 1963, which cost $44 million, which would be $295 million by today's standards.

But the most expensive movie ever is Pirates of the Caribbean: At World's End, which cost $305 million.

223. **George Lucas directed the original Star Wars trilogy.**

George did direct the original Star Wars in 1977.

But Irvin Kershner directed the second movie. He made such classics as...that James Bond film that is not even an official James Bond movie. And who could forget...Robocop 2.... Huh...

Well what about the third movie?

Richard Marquand directed Return of the Jedi.

Look, I'll level with you. I consider myself a film buff...but I've never heard of any of this guys movies.

224. **Mickey Mouse's first movie was Steamboat Willie in 1928.**

Mickey's first appeared in Plane Crazy and The Gallopin' Gaucho several months before Steamboat Willie. They didn't do well because Mickey wasn't likeable in these cartoons.

Disney revised the character as the loveable mouse that we know today for Steamboat Willie and Mickey Mouse's legacy was born.

225. **Every Hollywood movie now is a remake.**

Do you remember when movies were clever and epic like Ben-Hur, The Ten Commandments and The Wizard of Oz? You don't see anyone try to remake them because they're classics.

But they are all remakes. The 1955 Ben-Hur that won eleven Oscars is the second remake of the story inspired by the 1880 novel. The first Ben-Hur movie was in 1907 and the second one was the 1925 (the same year as the original Wizard of Oz.)

The original Ten Commandments was in 1923.

The "original" versions of Frankenstein, The Mummy and Dracula in the 1930s are also remakes.

PEOPLE

226. **Vincent Van Gogh's surname is pronounced "Van Goff" or "Van Go."**
Not even close. It's pronounced "Van Hhhuckh."

227. **Hannibal defeated his enemy with elephants.**
Hannibal did cross The Alps with elephants but he defeated King Eumenes by firing pots of snakes in the Battle of Eurymedon.

228. **Judges have gavels.**
Auctioneers have gavels. Television judges like Judge Judy use gavels for entertainment value but judges have never used them.

229. **The most dangerous job in the world is a firefighter.**
Alaskan crab fishing is the most dangerous job. For every 100,000 crab fishermen, 128 will die.

230. **Betty Crocker existed.**
Betty Crocker is a brand name and trademark of American Fortune 500 corporation General Mills. She never existed.

231. **Tokyo Rose existed.**
Tokyo Rose was said to be a protestor during World War II that made anti-war radio announcements.
But she never existed. Tokyo Rose was a general name American soldiers gave to any English-speaking Japanese women on the radio. The term "Tokyo Rose" was used so often that the general populace assumed that she was a real person.

232. **Sun Tzu existed.**
Sun Tzu's book The Art of War is written in a way that doesn't match the timeline as if it was written much later than it says.
Sun Tzu's name is never mentioned in history outside of this book. His book was probably a collaboration by many authors.

233. **Mavis Beacon existed.**
For over twenty years, Mavis Beacon has been an application on PC's to help people type. Mavis appears on the program as a posh, well-dressed, friendly, black woman that helps users.
People are very surprised to discover that she isn't based on a real person. She is simply an application character.

34. William Tell existed.

William Tell supposedly was an archer from Switzerland who shot an apple off the top of his son's head with his crossbow.

When I say this "supposedly" happen, I mean…it didn't happen. It's just a Swiss folklore story.

35. Nancy Drew's author Carole Keene existed.

There are several writers of the Nancy Drew books but they all use the pseudonym "Carole Keene."

36. Charles Manson is a mass murderer.

Manson has never killed a human being. He wasn't even present when his victims were killed. He manipulated people to kill others but never killed people himself (kind of like the murderer in the movie, Saw.)

37. Caesar Salad is named after Julius Caesar.

Caesar Cardini, a restaurant worker from Tijuana in Mexico, created the Caesar salad by accident.

On a busy Independence Day, his restaurant had little food left and he cobbled together what ingredients he had left to form the first Caesar salad.

38. Julius Caesar is so-named because his mother gave birth to him through Caesarean.

Caesar was born naturally. At the time of Caesar, caesarean births did happen, but the mothers always died. It has been recorded that Caesar's mother, Aurelia lived on for many years.

However, the month of July is derived from his name.

39. Julius Caesar wore wreaths on his head because he was the Emperor.

Caesar was incredibly vain and wore wreaths to hide his baldness. He also invented the comb over.

40. The great philosopher Plato's name was Plato.

Plato's name was Aritocles. Plato was his nickname. It means "wide."

His friends called him so because of his broad shoulders.

41. The Aztecs were called Aztecs.

Westerners invented the word "Aztecs" but they called themselves "Mexica."

242.   Genghis Khan was a huge, evil monster.

Khan did commit countless murders but he had an uncompromiseable moral code, which was ahead of its time. He banned adultery, theft, and even lying. He said that all people should respect each other's religious beliefs.

He's described as a seven foot tall monster but he was about 5ft 5 (average height for a Mongol.)

But he was surprisingly okay with killing 11% of EVERYONE ON EARTH! He is responsible for the death of 40 million people but he didn't like stealing or lies. I didn't peg Genghis as a "double-standard" kind of guy.

243.   Mozart's middle name was Amadeus.

Despite the play and movie of the same name, Johannes Chrysostomus Wolfgangus Theophilus Mozart was never called Amadeus. He had the nickname Amade, but never Amadeus.

244.   Rosa Parks was the first black woman to refuse to give up her seat on a bus to a white man in America.

Not only was Rosa not the first black woman to refuse to give up her seat in America, she wasn't even the first black woman to do it in her hometown.

Claudette Colvin was the first black woman to refuse to give up her seat. But black activists couldn't use her as an example for equality because she was a pregnant, unmarried teenager. Bigots would use her circumstances to undo all the good the Civil Rights Movement was trying to accomplish.

They needed a perfect candidate. Despite what many people believe, Rosa Parks was not just a sweet, old lady who refused to give up her seat because she was tired.

She was planted. Her refusal was pre-empted. She knew bigots would arrest her. The Civil Rights Movement knew she had a squeaky clean record. They predicted it would strengthen their cause, which it did.

245.   Robin Hood wore green.

In the main story of Robin Hood known as A Gest of Robyn Hode, he and his merry men wore red.

246.   Charles Darwin coined the phrase, "Survival of the Fittest."

Political theorist, Herbert Spencer came up with this idea. He was referencing himself as he was the only one of eight siblings to live to adulthood.

47.   There was uproar when Charles Darwin revealed his Survival of the Fittest theory.

This was not a particularly farfetched theory at the time because Darwin didn't concoct the idea from scratch. He was working off ideas from his competitor Robert Chambers as well as the Transmutation Theory. He combined these theories with his grandfather Erasmus's idea of a "common ancestor."

However, the first record of an evolution theory comes from Anaximander from Ancient Greece.

When Darwin put forward his theory the Church of England was quite supportive. They found it clinical and cold but an acceptable theory.

PLACES

48.   The Chernobyl nuclear reactor exploded in the 1980s rendering it useless.

Chernobyl was operational until December 2000. One reactor blew up. The other three worked perfectly. As dangerous as it was to continue working, there was just too much nuclear energy to go to waste. By sealing off the melted reactor with steel, engineers got back to work on the remaining three reactors.

49.   Tibet is a country.

Tibet hasn't been a country in over sixty years. What's even weirder is it was only a country for forty years (1913-1951.)

Tibet has existed for over a millennium but it wasn't its own country until the beginning of the twentieth century thanks to the Dalai Lama.

But after confronting the power of Mao, its sovereignty dissolved.

50.   Bagpipes came from Scotland.
Bagpipes are from Central Asia.

51.   Haggis is Scottish.
Haggis is Greek.

52.   Kilts are Scottish.
Kilts are Irish.

253. **Whisky is Scottish.**
Whisky is also Irish (obviously.)

254. **Porridge is Scottish.**
Porridge is Scandinavian.

255. **Chicken Tikka Masala is Indian AND DEFINITELY NOT SCOTTISH!**
Chicken Tikka Masala is Scottish.
Chicken Tikka originates from Bangladesh.
In Glasgow in the 1970s, a customer ordered chicken tikka but demanded it to be covered with gravy. The chef didn't have any, so he made a concoction with spices and tomato soup and chicken tikka masala was born.

256. **The driest place in the world is the Sahara Desert.**
The driest place is….Antarctica.
At this point, you might think, "Book….are you just making stuff up? Do you need to lie down?"
But "dry" doesn't mean hot or cold. It means one thing – rainfall
Although there are deserts that have 0.03cm of rain per year, Antarctica has 0.00cm per year. It hasn't rained there in millions of years.

257. **Gaelic is the Irish language spoken in Ireland.**
Gaelic was spoken before the Irish Potato Famine. Over the past century, Irish people now speak Gaeilge (pronounced Gwale-geh.)

258. **The poorest country is Somalia or Ethiopia.**
Neither of those nations are in the top ten poorest countries. The poorest country is Congo with an annual average of $348 per capita.

259. **The most dangerous country in the world is America.**
The US is the eight most dangerous country with 15,000 murders per year.
India has the most with nearly 43,000 murders per year.

260. **The country that drinks the most is Ireland.**
Belarus, Hungary, Ukraine, Romania, and Russia drink far more
But the country that drinks the most is Moldova.

61. **The country that commits suicide the most is Japan.**
Japan has the eighth highest suicide rate.
Lithuania has the highest suicide rate at thirty-four people for every 100,000.

62. **The most dangerous city in the world is Baghdad.**
Is it Detroit? New Orleans? Rio de Janeiro? Mogadishu? Somewhere in Mexico? Surely Capetown?
Nope. The highest murder and crime rate is in Caracas in Venezuela. It has 130 murders and 537 kidnappings for every 100,000 inhabitants.

63. **The country that lives the longest is Japan.**
The average life expectancy in Japan is eighty-three.
The average life expectancy in Monaco is ninety years old. That's not even old over there. That's considered normal. So if you died at eighty-eight, people would say, "Such a shame...taken before his time. The good always die so young."

64. **Crucifixion hasn't been a means of torture for centuries.**
To this day, Sudan still carries out crucifixion.

65. **Egypt has more pyramids than any other country.**
Nope. And it's not Peru or Mexico either.
It's Sudan again with at least thirty-five.

66. **The Nile is mostly in Egypt.**
The Nile is in Egypt but most of the Nile is in...you guessed it....Sudan. Again. Third time in a row, and the second time they've stolen the thunder from Egypt. How come Sudan never gets any credit?

67. **The biggest pyramid in the world is Giza.**
It's not (but thankfully it's not in Sudan.)
Cholula is an Aztec Pyramid and it is the biggest pyramid in the world.
Giza is the tallest however but Cholula has the biggest mass as it is occupies 4.3 million cubit yards compared to Giza's pyramid, which occupies 3.4 million.

268.   **"Blood is thicker than water," means "family is stronger than anything."**
This means the exact opposite of what you think it means.
This quote means, "The blood your soldiers spill in order to keep you alive means you are closer to your comrades than to your own family."

269.   **"Curiosity killed the cat" means "knowing too much can be dangerous."**
Ben Johnson created this phrase in 1598 in the play, Every Man in His Humor. But the phrase was originally "care killed the cat," not curiosity.
In modern terms, it means, "Caring too much about something can kill you." Simply put, "Worrying can kill you."

270.   **Tarzan says, "Me Tarzan, you Jane" in the original 1932 movie, Tarzan, the Ape Man.**
Untrue.

271.   **Dracula says, "I vant to suck your blood." in the movie Dracula.**
Nonsense.

272.   **George W. Bush has said a lot of hilariously stupid things.**
I have seen posters with idiotic Bush quotes like,
 "Time for the human race to enter the solar system."
"For NASA, space is still a high priority."
"The future will be better tomorrow."
These quotes and many more are from former Vice-President, Dan Quayle.
If any politician said something silly at the time, Bush got the blame. Some quotes were jokes by satirical magazines and weren't to be taken seriously.
Bush did say very stupid things. But a lot of politicians and presidents (and people) did too.

273.   **Harry Callahan says, "Do you feel lucky punk?" in the movie, Dirty Harry.**
The exact quote from Harry Callahan is, "Ask yourself one question, "Do I feel lucky?" Well, do you, punk?"

274.   {SPOILERS – DO NOT READ THIS FACT IF YOU HAVEN'T SEEN STAR WARS EPISODE V THE EMPIRE STRIKES BACK. YOU HAVE BEEN WARNED.}

Vader says, "Luke, I am your father." In the movie Star Wars Episode V, The Empire Strikes Back.
This is the dialogue from the movie.
Vader: Obi-Wan never told you what happened to your father.
Luke: He told me enough. He told me YOU killed him.
Vader: No. I am your father.
Please debate this dialogue with any Star Wars fan. It will melt their brain.

275.   **Obi-Wan Kenobi says, "May the force be with you" in Star Wars.**
If you have a friend who's obsessed with Star Wars, who can quote it effortlessly and knows what a Gamorean is, ask them, "When does Obi-Wan say, "May the force be with you." and watch your friend's brain explode.
Hans Solo says it before Luke heads to the Death Star.

276.   **"Take the road not taken," means "forge your own path instead of following everybody else."**
Robert Frost's poem, The Road Not Taken is often misunderstood. The second stanza states that both roads are "worn, really about the same."
Frost believed people find significance in random decisions. He references this when talking about his friend, Edward Thomas by saying, "Whichever road he went, he would be sorry he didn't go the other."

277.   **There are loads of quotes on the Internet by famous people.**
I've seen dozens of quotes on Twitter and Facebook by Morgan Freeman, Nelson Mandela, Abraham Lincoln and countless others. But a lot of them are fabricated. Some people online want to make a point and they put a picture of a historical figure or a celebrity beside it as if it gives the quote more meaning.
If you see a dubious quote like this on the Internet, verify it before you share it and retweet to all of your friends.

RELIGION

278.   Adam and Eve ate an apple in the Garden of Eden.

The Bible doesn't specify what fruit they ate. The idea of an apple probably became popularized from an old painting.

The Hebrew word in one of the translations is *tapuach,* which means "scented fruit." It is more likely it was an apricot, fig, or quince

279.   Noah built a huge ship according to the Bible.

It's not called Noah's Boat. It's an Ark. Have you ever heard someone go on holiday on an Ark?

Drawings of the Ark make it look like a ship with a steering mast. Noah didn't sail the Ark in the Bible. Where would he go? The beach for the weekend?

Ark means "box" or "chest." It was a huge wooden mass that he needed to stay in to wait for the flood to pass.

280.   Noah took two of every kind of animal.

It says in Genesis 7:2 "Of every clean beast, thou shalt take to thee by sevens, the male and his female, and of the beasts are not clean by two, the male and his female."

The unclean animals that are taken in twos were the animals Jews were not allowed to eat. The clean animals were any other animals that were edible.

281.   The Bible has Ten Commandments.

More like 613.

Okay, I'm not going to list every commandment but the Bible says that it is forbidden to practice witchcraft, wizardry, or…eating camels.

But you might think there are ten official Commandments. Surely the Commandments that Moses possessed were on the two tablets that God gave him.

They weren't called The Ten Commandments because there were thirteen.

Several of them are similar so it's common to bundle several commandments into one.

"Thou shalt not covet thy neighbors house" is usually combined with "Thou shalt not steal."

"Keep the Sabbath holy," "don't work on Sunday" and "work all other days of the week" are three commandments but are often clumped together just to round off the commandments to ten.

82.   The worst Commandment to break is Thou Shalt Not Kill.

The Commandments were originally written in order of importance.

The first five Commandments are-

a) Thou shalt not have other false Gods before me.

b) Thou shalt not take the Lord's name in vain.

c) Keep the Sabbath Holy.

d) Honor your father and mother.

e) Thou shalt not kill.

When the Commandments were written, killing was considered the fifth worst offence!

83.   Samson had his hair cut off by Delilah in the Bible.

Delilah's servant committed the deed.

84.   In the Bible, Mary Magdalene was a prostitute.

Mary Magdalene is barely mentioned in the Bible but she is never associated with prostitution.

85.   The Number of the Beast is 666 and he is the Antichrist

That's a mistranslation. It's 616. This was corrected shortly after the Bible was written but this idea has lingered ever since (probably because it has a better ring to it.)

The Beast in the Bible isn't a person. It is literally a Beast. It is a huge monster with ten horns, seven heads and ten crowns that comes out of the sea.

There is a False Prophet mentioned in the Book of Revelations who some people believe is the Antichrist but it is the Beast that bears the number 616.

But this isn't a reference to the Antichrist because...

86.   The Antichrist is mentioned in the Bible.

The Antichrist IS mentioned in the Bible four times.

But the Antichrist is not the son of Satan or a person destined to create Armageddon. It is a person who doesn't believe in Christ's divinity.

Here's exactly what it says in 2 John 1:7 –"Many deceivers, who do not acknowledge Jesus Christ as coming in the flesh, have gone out into the world. Any such person is the deceiver and the Antichrist."

Saying a person is an Antichrist is like saying a person is anti-war. It means you do not believe in Christ's divinity. It doesn't mean you're the spawn of Satan.

287. Angels are described in the Bible as beautiful beings that play harps and have white wings and a halo above their head.

There are many types of Biblical angels; angels, archangels, virtues, thrones, powers, cherubim, and seraphim.

When I mentioned "cherubim" you would probably think of the cute babies you see in artwork, especially in the Sistine Chapel.

This is what it says in Ezekiel 10:14 –

"Each of the cherubim had four faces: One face was that of a cherub, the second face of a human being, the third face of a lion, and the fourth the face of an eagle." That's…scary.

The throne angels are described as "wheels within wheels" with the wheel rims completely covered in eyes. ……That sounds terrifying

Painters wanted to sculpt, draw, and paint something peaceful and beautiful. Therefore the cherubim and thrones were….revised.

The "plucking harps" image was first mentioned in John Milton's Paradise Lost.

288. Hell is described as a fiery prison ruled by The Devil.

There is no suggestion that Satan rules Hell. That idea comes from Paradise Lost again.

When God banishes Lucifer, it is described in 2 Peter 2:4 as, "God did not spare the angels when they sinned, but sent them to hell, putting them into chains of darkness to be held for judgment."

Satan is not the king of Hell. He's a prisoner.

There are no "nine levels of Hell" mentioned. That idea was first depicted in Dante's Inferno.

289. The Devil is described in the Bible as a horned, red beast with hoofed feet, a spiked tail, and a scepter.

This image was taken from the Greco-Roman satyr Pan. Pan looks similar to a goat because of his hooves, horns and tail (he also had a trident which was a symbol of power, not evil.)

Pan was a God of fertility. The Roman Catholic Church was not a fan of "embracing fertility" because it made women look strong. The Church said this depiction of Pan was evil.

The Bible never states Satan's exact appearance. It implies that he is beautiful. He is described as "masquerading as an angel of light" and he is called "the son of the morning," and "a beautiful cherub."

Wait…isn't he described as a snake in the Garden of Eden? The Bible doesn't say the snake is Satan. It's just a snake…that talks….

The idea of Satan tricking people to steal souls is also never mentioned in the Bible. This idea comes from the play Faust by Goethe.

90. Lent lasts for forty days.

Lent starts on Ash Wednesday and ends on Good Friday and it is never shorter than forty-four days.

91. The Bible mentions the Holy Grail.

The Bible mentions that Jesus used a cup in the Last Supper but it doesn't suggest this cup is now enchanted.

This is like if the Bible mentioned that Jesus sat in a chair and now there is a Holy Chair secretly hidden somewhere in the world. Which there isn't.

92. Three wise men visited Jesus as a newborn in a stable.

Matthew 2:1 says, "Now when Jesus was born in Bethlehem of Judaea in the days of Herod the king, behold, there came wise men from the east to Jerusalem."

Wise men. Not three wise men. Just wise men.

It continues in Matthew 2:1 with, "And when they were come into the house, they saw the young child with Mary his mother, and fell down, and worshipped him."

So not only does the Bible say it was a house and not a stable but it says that Jesus was a young child, not a baby.

For extra confusion, Luke 2 says they were shepherds, not wise men. Who would've ever thought religion would be confusing?

93. Jesus was a lonely child.

Jesus' brothers are mentioned in Matthew 12:46, Luke 8:19, John 7:1-10, Acts 1:14, Galatians 1:19, and Mark 3:31.

Jesus had four brothers: James, Joseph, Simon, and Judah (Matthew 13:55).

The Bible also tells us that Jesus had sisters in Matthew 13:56, but they are not named or numbered.

SCIENCE

94. The speed of light is 186,000km per second.

186,000km per second is the maximum speed of light and it is only possible in a vacuum in space. If there is an object in the way, light will slow down as it passes through it. The denser the object, the slower light becomes. Researchers have slowed light down to just thirty-eight miles per hour by making it pass through dense materials. This means you could outcycle light.

295.   **Lightning doesn't strike the same area twice.**
        The Earth is billions of years old. I can imagine that a few of the same places have been struck numerous times, especially if lightning strikes 8.6 million times a day (that's a hundred per second.)
        Many skyscrapers get struck hundreds of times every year. Some spots can be struck twice in the same storm.

296.   **Electroconvulsive therapy (ECT) is an inhumane treatment.**
        ECT is one of the most effective therapies for disorders like bipolar or schizophrenia. Results show a 60-70% remission in people suffering depression.

297.   **Clones look identical.**
        If you cloned an animal ten times, you may have ten different looking creatures. A cat called Rainbow had a clone called Copycat (what else?) They looked nothing alike in color or pattern.

298.   **Meth can be blue just like in the television show, Breaking Bad.**
        It's impossible for meth to be blue. Its chemical disposition limits its coloring; changing this would have an adverse effect on its potency.
        Vince Gilligan, the creator of Breaking Bad, decided to make the drugs blue so they stood out more on screen and on posters.

299.   **The Large Hadron Collider is pointless and a dangerous.**
        The Large Hadron Collider has advanced our understanding of particle physics far more than other research.
        Big deal. What does particle physics even do?
        It fights cancer. Scans, X-Rays, treatments, injections, radiotherapy, predicting cancer, fighting cancer, curing cancer, and killing cancer are all possible because of that Collider.

300.   **Humanity evolved from apes.**
        Charles Darwin never suggested we came from apes. Those that dismiss evolution use this misunderstanding by saying, "If we came from apes, why do apes still exist?" Darwin said apes and humans had a common ancestor.
        This common ancestor went down multiple genetic paths; one of them was apes, one of them was humans, and other paths that didn't survive like Neanderthals. But that is not the only misconception people made about evolution.

01. Evolution is the process of animals adapting to their surroundings within a few generations to survive.

Ironically this is what people used to believe before Darwin came along.

Mutations are random. If the world suddenly became far colder, your genes wouldn't just adapt to cold. Of all the millions of animals in the world, there will be a few here and there who are more genetically resistant to cold, and they would survive because they were more adaptable.

That doesn't mean they are "better." They just happened to be suited to those specific circumstances. If the planet suddenly became far hotter, they would be the first to die.

02. MMR vaccines can cause autism.

It was suggested that 1 in 110 people injected with the MMR vaccine would get autism.

Vaccines today will make you immune to diphtheria, whooping cough, pneumonia, mumps, hepatitis A and B, chicken pox, smallpox, rubella, polio, tetanus, meningitis, and other viruses.

If hypothetically, vaccines had a less than 1% chance of causing autism, the chances of getting one of the above would be almost guaranteed because people would avoid using them (my mother didn't get the Salk vaccine and she's had polio for over fifty years.)

So it is unquestionably healthier to get vaccinated even if vaccines could potentially cause autism.

But the vaccines DON'T cause autism! This argument has been closed for twenty years.

Andrew Wakefield was a former doctor (he's not anymore and you'll see why in a minute) who claimed there was a link with vaccines and autism.

Six years later, it turned out that his theory of vaccines causing autism was so inconsistent, he was stripped of his ability to practice medicine.

03. Einstein repeatedly failed math's in school.

He didn't. Because he's Einstein.

He mastered differential and integral calculus at fifteen.

That's the opposite of flunking math.

04. Einstein won a Nobel Prize for his Theory of General Relativity.

Einstein won the Nobel Prize for his lesser-known theory on the photoelectric effect of light.

305.   Mercury is the only metal that is liquid at room temperature.
Caesium, francium, rubidium, bromine, and gallium are also liquid metals at room temperature.

306.   If you turn lights on and off often in an attempt to save electricity, it uses more electricity than leaving it on.
The idea behind this misconception is that most of the electricity is used in turning on the light. But this is untrue. It's like believing turning a car on and off over and over again will use up more fuel than travelling hundreds of miles.

SPACE

307.   Being an astronaut would be awesome.
Astronauts suffer muscle atrophy, bone deterioration (especially in the spine and neck,) and a damaged cardiovascular system. A lack of clean water creates lots of bacteria leading to illness which you can't fight because your immune system is weakened.
Psychologically, space can be scary. Insomnia, rage, depression, and psychosis are not uncommon.

308.   Meteorites are extremely hot.
A meteorite is -270 Celsius (nearly absolute zero.) When it passes through our atmosphere, it becomes very hot. But the core of the meteorite remains freezing.
As it passes out of the Earth's atmosphere, the cold core will revert the whole meteorite surface to freezing within minutes.

309.   If you travelled into an asteroid belt, you would see loads of asteroids just like Star Wars.
There's hundreds of thousands of asteroids but each asteroid is about three million miles apart from each other. You can travel in and out of an asteroid belt without seeing one single asteroid.

310.   The seasons of the year are based on the distance Earth is from the Sun.
Earth is always the same distance from the Sun. If we were any closer, we would burn. Any further, we would freeze.
The seasons are caused by the 23-degree axial tilt (obviously.) We tilt towards the Sun in the summer and we tilt away in the winter.

11. NASA have sent robots to space recently.
The Opportunity rover landed on Mars in 2003. It was expected to last three months. It's still operational today.

12. Spaceships burn on re-entry because of the atmosphere.
It's not the atmosphere that creates the heat, it's the compression. As the craft hurtles through the sky, the air around it compresses and heats up and it doesn't have a chance to cool until it slows down.

13. A comet moves in one direction so its tail is facing the other direction.
A comet's tail is created by solar wind so no matter what direction a comet is moving in, the tail will always face away from the Sun.

14. The first animal in space was a dog.
No, and it wasn't a chimp either. It was a fruit fly.
Fruit flies were sent into space in 1946 to test radioactive exposure to gauge if humans could survive space.
Eleven years later, Laika the dog was sent into space.

15. The Sun is a huge star.
The Sun is so enormous that 1.3 million Earths would fit in it. But the Sun is pretty small compared to other stars. It's categorized as a dwarf star.
Canis Majoris is the largest star. It's a billion times bigger than the Sun.

16. The Sun is red or yellow.
When you see pictures of the Sun, you are looking at a nuclear explosion emanating from every part of the Sun. The Sun itself is actually white.

17. If the Sun suddenly moved, everyone on Earth would freeze.
The Sun isn't stationary. It is moving throughout the Solar System. But we have nothing to worry about because Earth is caught in the Sun's gravitational field. Wherever the Sun moves, the Earth will automatically remain exactly the same distance away from it.

318. The universe is mostly black.

Astrologists have studied 200,000 galaxies and when they condensed and compressed the color of every galaxy, it always comes back as the same color – beige. So there you go, the universe is beige. I wrote this book and even I find it hard to believe that one.

319. We see every side of the moon at some point.

The same side of the moon is always facing us. We can never see the other side, which is called The Dark Side of the Moon.

320. The moon is spherical.

The moon is shaped like an egg. It looks round to us because we always see the same side of it.

321. You can see the Great Wall of China from the Moon.

You can barely see anything from the moon. You can barely see the Great Wall from Earth's orbit and the conditions have to be exact.

There's never a time where the Great Wall is the only landmark you can see from space.

322. Earth has only one moon.

To quote Alan Davies in the show QI, "We have only one moon. It's called The Moon."

In the same show, the host, Stephen Fry countered by saying that we have one visible moon (called Luna) but there is another smaller moon far away that circles the Earth called Cruitne.

This gets even more complicated when two years later on the same show, Fry said that they have found three more moons circulating Earth (and it has suggested that there's more.)

323. The moon affects the tides.

It does, but it is not the only thing that affects the tides. The Sun has partial responsibility too.

324. When a star dies, it turns into a black hole.

Only large stars turn into black holes when they die. When our Sun dies in a billion years or so, it will collapse into a white dwarf.

325. Black holes are funnel shaped.

In diagrams, black holes look 2D to give us a small understanding of what happens to the matter it absorbs.

However, a black hole is not flat, it's a sphere. It's not black either, it's invisible. It works like a planet but with far more gravity.

26. Nothing can escape a black hole.

There is an area near a black hole called the event horizon. This is the "no turning back" region. Once you are close enough to a black hole, you're going into it and there's nothing you can do to stop it.

Stephen Hawking famously said this decades ago. No one is going to contest one of the most brilliant minds in history so it was accepted as fact.

But years later, he admitted he was wrong. After further calculations, he realized that black holes create ripples, which are strong enough to knock matter out of the event horizon.

Even the smartest guy in the world can get it wrong.

27. Jupiter is slightly larger than Saturn.

Jupiter is so big that every planet could fit in it two and a half times.

28. Ballpoint pens don't work in zero gravity so NASA spent $1.5 million perfecting a Space Pen. Russians just used pencils.

Yes, a Space Pen was invented for over a million dollars. But NASA didn't pay a penny for it.

Paul C. Fisher of Fisher Pen Co. did this of his own free will. He was offering his services and wasn't asked by NASA for help. He created the Space Pen and gave it to NASA.

But why didn't they just use pencils?

Pencil tips can flake off and the smallest form of debris in a space capsule can be hazardous because it could float into an astronaut's eye or into electric equipment.

The Americans and the Russians both used pencils originally and they both switched to the Space Pen once it was created.

29. People cared about the Moon landing.

Do you remember a few years ago when scientists found the Higgs-boson? What year was it? Date? Time?

Scientists say the Higgs-boson is arguably the greatest scientific discovery ever. Not of our lifetime. Ever. Do you know what it is or what it does?

Your answer is probably, "No, and I don't care."

That's how most people felt about the moon landing.

The common consensus in America at the time was that there was a Cold War and a threat of nuclear annihilation. The last thing people needed was America and Russia competing against each other to see who can go to a big dead rock first.

UNSOLVED MYSTERIES

330. **Which came first, the chicken or the egg?**
The chicken. Mystery solved. Good night folks.
Wait, you probably want an explanation................fine...
The chicken egg has a protein compound called ovocledidin-17.
This can only be found in one place on Earth – the ovary of a chicken.
No protein means no egg, which means the chicken must've come
first.

331. **No one knows who built the Easter Island Heads.**
Easter Island used to have inhabitants called the Rapa Nui. This
primitive tribe constructed massive statues 400 years ago. Nobody
knows why but it was unquestionably their top priority.
But if they built the statues, why aren't the Rapa Nui around?
They cut down all of the trees to roll the boulders they needed
to build the statues. After building a thousand statues, they had
destroyed their entire forest. They cut down all of the trees so quickly
it stripped the soil of nutrients so nothing would grow. With no food,
they resorted to cannibalism. After thirty years, they were nearly
extinct.
All because they thought it would be cool to build some heads.

332. **Spiritual people can see other people's aura.**
If you ever heard of a person who claimed to see auras and
would say "that person has a nice orange aura" or "she has a negative
red aura," it's easy to assume this person is lying. But they may not
be. A person who claims to see auras genuinely might see them.
There are many reasons people see distorted colors. A person might
see distorted colors from the most basic conditions like eye burns,
epilepsy or a migraine.
But these are disorders that come and go. What about people
who always see auras? Are they psychic? No. It is likely they suffer
from synesthesia. This is a disorder where senses like sound, sight
and taste get mixed up. A person with synesthesia might hear a dog
bark and this might cause them to taste chocolate and smell tulips.
They might get this sensation every single time they hear a dog bark.
If a synesthete sees a person, a sound or smell might force
their brain to see this person in a specific color. Some people who
genuinely believe they see auras actually have undiagnosed
synesthesia.

333.   Area 51 is a top-secret location where the American government have alien UFOS, including the flying saucers from Roswell.

Area 51 totally exists. It's not a secret. It's in Nevada, 83 miles north-northwest of Las Vegas. You can find it on Google Earth.

But it used to be top-secret. A tourist can't just walk up to it. After all, it is a government building. Simply put, Area 51 is where American government builds and tests new military craft and weaponry.

So why is it in such a remote area? If you were to build a new ship with weapons that haven't been fully tested, you would want as much space as possible for them to fly around in.

334.   El Dorado was an ancient city of gold.

The ancient tribe, the Muisca covered their chieftain in gold dust when he was elected. Spaniards misunderstood this and assumed there was a city where gold was so plentiful that they could throw it at each other.

When the Spaniards asked the natives of this secret golden city, they encouraged the Spaniards that it existed miles away hoping that the greedy, gold-obsessed Spaniards would leave their civilization in peace.

335.   Amelia Earhart mysteriously vanished.

This mystery was solved four years after Earhart went missing. There's nothing particular suspicious about her disappearance. Her plane crashed near an island in Kiribati and most of her skeleton was found. The skeleton matched her measurements. They also found her equipment. Most importantly, the island was uninhabited. Amelia was the only person on it, alive or dead.

336.   The ancient Mayans disappeared into thin air overnight.

The Mayan's disappearance wasn't sudden. Their numbers dwindled to extinction over hundreds of years thanks to civil wars, droughts, and deforestation which destroyed all of their resources.

337.   Ships mysteriously vanish in The Bermuda Triangle.

When is the last time you've heard of a plane or ship going missing in The Bermuda Triangle? The last time any major vehicle went missing there is fifteen years ago.

Statistically, there are more dangerous areas in the world that have taken more lives through non-supernatural phenomena like storms and violent waves.

338. We have yet to find The Missing Link, the common ancestor.

There is no ONE link. Critics of evolution argue by saying there is no Missing Link between our original ancestor and us.

But there is. It's called Homo erectus. But who is the link between our original ancestor and Homo erectus? Homo habilius. Before you ask, the next one is called Australopithecus.

The differences between Homo erectus and Homo habilius is so slight, it's hard to say at which point do they stop being one species and start being another?

We have found numerous missing links. The most recent one was only four years ago. Scientists will uncover more in the near future. How many do we need to find to silence those who dismiss evolution? 50? 100? 1,000?

339. Atlantis may have existed.

Plato first mentioned Atlantis. He was a fiction writer.

You know who was the first person to mention Hogwarts? JK Rowling, She wrote Harry Potter, a fictional book. So Hogwarts probably doesn't exist either.

340. Aliens make crops circles.

Two people, a board, and a rope are all that is needed to form crop circles in just a few hours. The common method to construct a crop formation is to tie one end of a rope to an anchor point and the other end to a board, which a person uses to crush the plants.

It sounds too simple but Doug Bower and Dave Chorley have confessed to creating countless crop circles in the UK in 1991. Some people didn't believe them so they re-did the exact designs of famous crop circles throughout England and they matched perfectly.

341. Why is a raven like a writing desk?" is a riddle the Hatter says in Alice in Wonderland that never seems to have an answer

To quote the writer, Lewis Carroll, "Because it can produce a few notes, tho' they are very flat; and it is never put with the wrong end in front."

That answer…is terrible. Nobody understood this answer for over a century because there was a spelling error that was corrected but was meant to be left in. "Never" is meant to be spelt "nevar."

The end of the answer says, "It is **nevar** put with the wrong end in front."

End in front? Does it mean read "nevar" backwards? What does it read? Raven.

342.   No one knows how Stonehenge was built.

It's not just the construction of Stonehenge that's a problem. It's the location. Why would anyone drag enormous rocks for miles to the middle of nowhere? How?

A retired construction worker from Michigan called Wally Wallington (I swear that's his real name) built his own Stonehenge. By himself. In his garden. Just to see if he could.

You might think, "That doesn't count. Even if he is one person, he still did it with modern technology and cranes and bulldozers."

No. He did this with what was available at the time of the Stone Age; simplistic pulleys and levers and pivots made of rope and stone. If this guy can do it alone, surely dozens of men can do it.

"But he did this in his garden," you might think. "The Stonehenge makers dragged rocks for miles."

They didn't. Stonehenge was in the center of the largest Stone Age civilization ever discovered.

343.   The Loch Ness monster might exist.

This idea became popularized after a photograph was taken in 1934 (even though the photographer Robert Wilson admitted he forged it.)

But I have one main argument. It's not the fact that it's supposed to be a prehistoric creature, its limited procreativity or its ability to survive for millions of years. It's simply this – What would it eat?

An animal that size would have to eat a staggering amount of food. Every single day. A blue whale couldn't physically live in a lake because it would run out of food very quickly. If a Loch Ness Monster suddenly appeared in Loch Ness tomorrow, it would completely run out of food in a few days.

344.   Déjà vu is a mystery.

We have 100,000 neurons firing in our brain at any one time. Some of them are relaying what is happening now and what has happened in the past.

Since we have so many neurons, it's common that one will send a signal the wrong way. So when your neuron is supposed to send a signal to tell you what is happening now, it might accidentally send one saying that what you are currently doing is in the past.

These mixed signals will make you feel like that what you are doing has already happened. This tends to happen when you are not concentrating like when you are doing some tedious task like cooking or cleaning.

345.   There are theories how the pyramids were built but inconsistencies in each one.

The blocks were put on top of each other using wide ramps. This much has been known for some time. But researches couldn't fathom how the Egyptians moved countless blocks so quickly.

Unless they could somehow make the blocks slide.

But how? They simply used water. Wet sand creates a firmer surface and reduces friction, which drastically reduced the workload. The blocks would slide through the sand and everything could be built faster and more efficiently.

346.   The Illuminati exist.

Nesta Webster was a British anti-Semitic propagandist in the 1920s. She hated the Jews so much that she took every chance she could to say they were responsible for all of history's atrocities.

Of course this is impossible. There is no way any group of people could be responsible for all of the horrific things in history...unless of course there was an overelaborate interconnected network of secret societies spanning the globe controlling everything....

But that still wouldn't work. She couldn't just make up a cult and everybody would believe it, right?

And one day, she heard of The Illuminati. The Illuminati was founded in 1776 to oppose superstition, dogma, and indoctrination. But the society was outlawed and disbanded....nine years later. The Illuminati existed on Earth for nine whole years. That's it.

Webster combined her hatred of Jews with this group saying that the Jews secretly resurrected the society. This idea was easy to believe, as there was already a conspiracy that the Illuminati caused the French Revolution.

She didn't make up The Illuminati. You can find records of them in history. But she made up the idea that they secretly rule the planet. The idea of The Illuminati controlling the world has only been around for less than a century. Nobody thought that even when they existed! Since they no longer existed, the real Illuminati couldn't defend themselves.

This was easier to believe that anyone can imagine. Many people don't know the difference between any secret societies so a lot of conspiracy theorists assume societies like The Freemasons, The Opus Dei, and The Illuminati are all interconnected.

WORDS

47. **"I'll be back in a jiffy," means, "I'll be back very soon."**

A jiffy is an actual unit of measurement.

You are actually saying is, "I'll be back before light has travelled one centimeter which is thirty-three picoseconds or one trillionth of a second." That doesn't have the same ring to it.

48. **"I haven't see you in yonks" means "I haven't seen you in ages!"**

A yonk is British slang for "donkey's year." Donkey's live about 3½ times less than humans. So a yonk is 365÷3.5= 104 days. So three months and fourteen days is one yonk.

I have to calculate a donkey's mortality using mathematics to comprehend a British slang word. How did this become my job???

49. **"Mano-a-mano" means "man-to-man."**

If a guy picks a fight with you and he says, "You and me, outside now. Mano-a-mano. Man-to-man," you should correct them by saying "Sorry. 'Mano-a-mano' means 'hand-to-hand' in Portuguese, Spanish, and Italian. Not man-to-man."

The guy who's about to beat you to a pulp will probably appreciate you correcting him.

50. **Wikipedia is pronounced like "wi-ki-pee-dee-a."**

"Wee-kee-pee-dee-a" is the correct way which I never use.

51. **Mt Everest is pronounced "Ever-est."**

Mt Everest is named after George Everest who surveyed the mountain when Tenzing originally climbed it. But his name was pronounced "ee-ver-est."

52. **"Goodbye" means "farewell."**

Goodbye is an abbreviation of "God be with ye." It has been used since the fourteenth century.

53. **"Nimrod" means "idiot."**

Nimrod was the greatest hunter in the Bible.

In a Looney Tunes cartoon, Elmer Fudd tried to shoot Bugs Bunny and missed. Bugs sarcastically said, "Nice shooting Nimrod!!"

Kids didn't have a clue what this obscure reference meant so they assumed "Nimrod" meant "idiot."

354.   "Chronic" means "painful."
"Chronic" means long-term pain. A chronic back pain is a permanent pain.

355.   "Larvae" is pronounced "lar-vay."
There are two ways to say "larvae." It's can be pronounced "lar-vai" or "lar-vee" but never "lar-vay" (even though I have never heard be pronounced any way except the wrong way.

The Ten Most Bizarre Misconceptions

356.   Leprosy makes your flesh rot and drop off.
Leprosy doesn't exist. There is no disease that makes body parts fall off.
(I know it's late in the book, but I hope it's still shocking you.)
Hansen's disease has been misunderstood as leprosy.
Hansen's disease damages a person's skin and nerve endings in their hands and feet. This can make "lepers" immune to pain in their fingers and toes.
Sufferers of this disease repeatedly injure their hands and feet without realizing it, which leads to horrific infections. This can lead to amputations but your fingers or toes could never fall off from the disease directly.
Our ancestors were so scared of leprosy that for millennia, everyone with skin abnormalities (psoriasis, eczema, or rashes) were cast out of their villages.
Even those who were banished from their home for having a mild skin disorder would genuinely believe they had leprosy and surviving with it for decades was through pure luck.

357.   Alice in Wonderland is an allusion to hallucinogenic drugs.
The book's author, Lewis Carroll (or to use his real name, Charles Dodgson) has insisted that the book has nothing to do with drugs. The story is meant to show the absurdity of mathematics.
Mathematics had stayed pretty much the same for millennia. But it was at this time that mathematicians talked about what Carroll considered "absurd math's." This included lettered math's (x + y = z), imaginary numbers, and fractions larger than a whole (10/6ths.) This is why the most insane character, The Hatter (not The Mad Hatter) has a hat who's price tag says 10/6.
So the story is to show how weird math's is. Because that's wha kids like.

358.   You understand the Schrödinger's Cat theory.

This theory is the most famous example of quantum mechanics. Quantum physics is the idea that perception can affect reality and the universe's "rules" are not set in stone.

Erwin Schrodinger gave an example called Schrodinger's Cat. Imagine a cat is in a box. Poisonous gas is poured into the box. It has a 50/50 chance of killing the cat. When the box is opened, the cat will be alive or dead.

But in quantum physics, this only happens when the box is opened. Until we see the cat, the cat is alive AND dead.

Make sense? Yes? No? Doesn't matter because it's utter garbage. Erwin made it up as a joke to mock those who believed in quantum mechanics.

But quantum believers used his Cat theory to strengthen their own argument. It was like they said, "Look! Even Erwin has come to his senses and agrees that quantum physics is possible! He even gave us his own example." Erwin couldn't stop becoming the poster-child of a concept he despised.

This is like Hitler becoming the poster-child of Jewish equality.

359.   The appendix is the only part of the body that's useless.

Below are nine useless body parts.

a) Wisdom teeth

b) Auricular muscles allowed our ancestors to swivel their ears.

c) The third eyelid by our tear duct helped our ancestors see underwater.

d) The coccyx is what's left from when our ancestors had tails.

e) Male nipples are useless. All human beings start with nipples and never lose them.

f) Darwin's point is a flap of skin in our ear that does sod all.

g) The vomeronasal organ used to let our ancestors smell phernomes.

h) Erector pili give us goosebumps, which is useless unless we had more body hair.

i) Body hair

Ironically, the appendix isn't on the list. That's because appendix is useful! It creates antibodies and stores helpful bacteria. So you would be more prone to sickness if your appendix was removed.

360.   The English burned Joan of Arc at the stake for witchcraft.

The French burned her to death for dressing like a man.

The best way to understand this is using Al Capone as an example. Al Capone committed burglaries, beatings, and murder. But he was jailed for tax evasion because that was the only thing that the law could pin on him.

Joan of Arc had made herself a very powerful woman who committed many successful pre-emptive sieges. She was clad in armor and kept her hair short to look more masculine to be taken seriously by her men and her enemies.

Sadly, powerful women never went down well in Christian history.

The French wanted to get her out of the way anyway they could

She was accused of heresy before a French court and she admitted guilt (but only to avoid death.)

So since she couldn't be put to death unless she denied heresy, the court accused her of wearing men's clothes in battle. A woman dressing like a man is, "an abomination unto the Lord" according to Deuteronomy 22:5.

361.   There were Anthrax attacks shortly after 9/11 caused by al-Qaida.

Two senators and several news groups had anthrax sent to them in the mail shortly after September 11th. Five died and seventeen were hospitalized. $1 billion was spent to decontaminate any toxic agents. The American government desperately sought to find the culprit.

They found him in 2008. It was Dr. Bruce Ivins.

He was American.

The government discovered that the spores from the anthrax could only be tracked to his laboratory. He was the only person that had access.

He even sent the anthrax to people in his personal life not affiliated with the political world (but letters were also found to the senators and news groups mentioned above in his home or office.)

He was working unreasonable hours in his lab weeks before the attack. He was about to lose his funding because his foundation believed anthrax couldn't be used as an effective bio-weapon. He was never tried because he committed suicide as the government was honing in on him.

It seems to be a closed case. All evidence fitted perfectly. It may sound like a cover-up in an episode of 24 but no one else has ever taken credit for the attacks in thirteen years.

62.   The best place to discover a new species is in a jungle.

In 1971, a British biologist named Jennifer Owen found over five hundred types of wasp, fifteen of which had never been found in the UK before, and four of them were completely new species. She didn't do this in a jungle or in a subterranean cave or at the bottom of the ocean. She discovered these creatures in her garden.

If you want to uncover a new animal, you don't need to go halfway across the globe. Although you may not be able to notice the subtle differences between species, the average garden can have over 4,000 creatures and 250 plants.

63.   You see with your eyes.

Seriously? Where else are you expected to see things?

Well, how do you see dreams? Blind people have images in their head. How? If you picture an apple now, how does that work? Your eyes weren't looking at one, so how is it possible?

You see through the visual cortex. Your eyes assemble images by absorbing light and send it to your brain to register in your cortex.

This takes eighty milliseconds. So everything you see happened a split-second earlier than it seems.

You will never see the world the same again (through your visual cortex.)

64.   People understand how bicycles work.

Nobody in history has ever understood the science behind how a bicycle works. Not cyclists. Not scientists. Not NASA. Not physicists. Not Lance Armstrong. Ok, that's a bad example.

I know this sounds unbelievable. Even a child would believe he or she understands it. It has something to do with velocity and speed and gyroscopic effects or something, right? No. This has been debated for over a century and we are less certain than we were fifty years ago.

So there. Mankind split an atom before we could explain to a toddler how his or her bike works.

And the final misconception is...

365.   Fish exist.

      Stephen Jay Gould spent decades studying fish and discovered that they are genetically so different from each other that they are not a single species but thousands of separate species.

      A salmon has more genetic similarities to a camel than a hagfish.

      When we think of a fish, we mean, "any vertebrate that lives underwater that isn't a mammal or reptile."

      But this is a huge oversimplification. It's like saying every animal that lays an egg is a bird including all reptiles, the platypus, and….fish.

      This isn't even that farfetched. Hundreds of years ago, people believed seals, whales, hippos, and crocodiles were fish.

      So there you have it. There is no such thing as a fish.

      Whoever thought a book would end that way?

Printed in Great Britain
by Amazon